Illegal Immigration

Other Books of Related Interest:

Opposing Viewpoints Series
Culture Wars

Discrimination

National Security

Current Controversies
Developing Nations

Illegal Immigration

At Issue Series
Bilingual Education

Do Religious Groups in America Experience Discrimination?

Illegal Immigration

Paul Hina, Book Editor

GREENHAVEN PRESS
A part of Gale, Cengage Learning

Detroit • New York • San Francisco • New Haven, Conn • Waterville, Maine • London

GALE
CENGAGE Learning™

Christine Nasso, *Publisher*
Elizabeth Des Chenes, *Managing Editor*

© 2008 Greenhaven Press, a part of Gale, Cengage Learning.

Gale and Greenhaven Press are registered trademarks used herein under license.

For more information, contact:
Greenhaven Press
27500 Drake Rd.
Farmington Hills, MI 48331-3535
Or you can visit our Internet site at gale.cengage.com

For product information and technology assistance, contact us at

Gale Customer Support, 1-800-877-4253
For permission to use material from this text or product, submit all requests online at www.cengage.com/permissions

Further permissions questions can be emailed to permissionrequest@cengage.com

Articles in Greenhaven Press anthologies are often edited for length to meet page requirements. In addition, original titles of these works are changed to clearly present the main thesis and to explicitly indicate the author's opinion. Every effort is made to ensure that Greenhaven Press accurately reflects the original intent of the authors. Every effort has been made to trace the owners of copyrighted material.

Cover photograph reproduced by permission of Image copyright Christopher Penler, 2007. Used under license of Shutterstock.com.

LIBRARY OF CONGRESS CATALOGING-IN-PUBLICATION DATA

Illegal immigration / Paul Hina, book editor.
    p. cm. -- (Contemporary issues companion)
    Includes bibliographical references and index.
    ISBN-13: 978-0-7377-3948-0 (hardcover)
    ISBN-13: 978-0-7377-3949-7 (pbk.)
    1. Illegal aliens--United States--Juvenile literature. 2. United States--Emigration and immigration--Juvenile literature. I. Hina, Paul.
    JV6465.I448 2008
    325.73--dc22

                                                    2008006570

Printed in the United States of America
1 2 3 4 5 6 7 12 11 10 09 08

Contents

Foreword   **9**

Introduction   **12**

Chapter 1: Illegal Immigrants and Cultural Assimilation

1. Americans Are Divided Over Illegal Immigrants   **18**
   Pew Research Center for the People and the Press

2. The Government Should Have a Role   **27**
   in Encouraging Assimilation
   Karin Brulliard

3. Immigrants Are Assimilating Into   **34**
   American Culture
   Stephen J. Trejo

4. Immigrants Are Not Assimilating Into   **41**
   American Culture
   David Frum

5. Illegal Immigrants Are Dangerous for America   **48**
   R. Cort Kirkwood

Chapter 2: The Effects of Illegal Immigration on the American Economy

1. Immigrants Hurt the U.S. Economy   **58**
   Steven Malanga

2. Immigrants Help the U.S. Economy   **69**
   Daniel Griswold

3. Illegal Immigrants Are Costing Public   **77**
   Schools Too Much
   Jack Martin

4. Illegal Immigrants and Their Children   **85**
   Should Be Educated Despite Costs
   Houston Chronicle

5. Illegal Immigrants Are Abusing the
Public Health System
Alison Green and Jack Martin
92

6. Immigrants Are Not Causing the
Public Health System to Fail
Meredith L. King
105

Chapter 3: Political Responses to Illegal Immigration

1. Immigration Legislation Should Not
Reward Illegal Immigrants
Rep. Mike Pence
118

2. Immigration Legislation Should Not Punish
All Illegal Immigrants
Sen. Edward M. Kennedy
127

3. Amnesty for Illegal Immigrants Is Bad
for the United States
Kris W. Kobach
133

4. Amnesty for Illegal Immigrants Is Good
for the United States
Justin Akers Chacon
141

5. State Governments Are Forced to Act in the
Absence of Federal Immigration Reform
T.R. Reid
148

Chapter 4: Personal Perspectives on Illegal Immigration

1. My Family's Journey Across the U.S. Border
Faviola Rubio
155

2. Life as an Illegal Immigrant in America
Teresa Mendez
160

3. Patrolling the U.S. Border
Malia Politzer
168

4. A Minuteman Guards the Border   **178**
   Charlie LeDuff

5. Living on the Border   **183**
   Leo W. Banks

Organizations to Contact   **193**

Bibliography   **199**

Index   **204**

Foreword

In the news, on the streets, and in neighborhoods, individuals are confronted with a variety of social problems. Such problems may affect people directly: A young woman may struggle with depression, suspect a friend of having bulimia, or watch a loved one battle cancer. And even the issues that do not directly affect her private life—such as religious cults, domestic violence, or legalized gambling—still impact the larger society in which she lives. Discovering and analyzing the complexities of issues that encompass communal and societal realms as well as the world of personal experience is a valuable educational goal in the modern world.

Effectively addressing social problems requires familiarity with a constantly changing stream of data. Becoming well informed about today's controversies is an intricate process that often involves reading myriad primary and secondary sources, analyzing political debates, weighing various experts' opinions—even listening to firsthand accounts of those directly affected by the issue. For students and general observers, this can be a daunting task because of the sheer volume of information available in books, periodicals, on the evening news, and on the Internet. Researching the consequences of legalized gambling, for example, might entail sifting through congressional testimony on gambling's societal effects, examining private studies on Indian gaming, perusing numerous websites devoted to Internet betting, and reading essays written by lottery winners as well as interviews with recovering compulsive gamblers. Obtaining valuable information can be time-consuming—since it often requires researchers to pore over numerous documents and commentaries before discovering a source relevant to their particular investigation.

Greenhaven's Contemporary Issues Companion series seeks to assist this process of research by providing readers with useful and pertinent information about today's complex issues. Each volume in this anthology series focuses on a topic of current interest, presenting informative and thought-provoking selections written from a wide variety of viewpoints. The readings selected by the editors include such diverse sources as personal accounts and case studies, pertinent factual and statistical articles, and relevant commentaries and over views. This diversity of sources and views, found in every Contemporary Issues Companion, offers readers a broad perspective in one convenient volume.

In addition, each title in the Contemporary Issues Companion series is designed especially for young adults. The selections included in every volume are chosen for their accessibility and are expertly edited in consideration of both the reading and comprehension levels of the audience. The structure of the anthologies also enhances accessibility. An introductory essay places each issue in context and provides helpful facts such as historical background or current statistics and legislation that pertain to the topic. The chapters that follow organize the material and focus on specific aspects of the book's topic. Every essay is introduced by a brief summary of its main points and biographical information about the author. These summaries aid in comprehension and can also serve to direct readers to material of immediate interest and need. Finally, a comprehensive index allows readers to efficiently scan and locate content.

The Contemporary Issues Companion series is an ideal launching point for research on a particular topic. Each anthology in the series is composed of readings taken from an extensive gamut of resources, including periodicals, newspapers, books, government documents, the publications of private and public organizations, and Internet Web sites. In these volumes, readers will find factual support suitable for use in reports, debates, speeches, and research papers. The anthologies also facilitate further research, featuring a book and periodical bibliography and a list of organizations to contact for additional information.

A perfect resource for both students and the general reader, Greenhaven's Contemporary Issues Companion series is sure to be a valued source of current, readable information on social problems that interest young adults. It is the editors' hope that readers will find the Contemporary Issues Companion series useful as a starting point to formulate their own opinions about and answers to the complex issues of the present day.

Introduction

As the debate over illegal immigration intensifies in the United States, many components of the issue compete for newspaper headlines. Issues include the economic impact of illegal immigration and the question of granting amnesty. One factor in the debate is the language gap that exists between the majority of illegal Spanish-speaking immigrants entering the country and English-speaking citizens. The question of language frames and informs many other conversations concerning illegal immigrants and their assimilation into the United States.

In the early 2000s, illegal immigration has become a flashpoint issue for politicians seeking to gain the support of their constituents. With the wind of the media and concerned citizens at their back, many state legislators have taken their own steps to address the one aspect of the cultural divide influencing all others: the ability to speak the English language. As of 2008, twenty-seven states have adopted English-only legislation, which prohibits the speaking of foreign languages in all statewide spheres. While these legislative steps affect certain state governments, they have no bearing on federal institutions.

That arrangement may change. The U.S. Congress has not been silent on the language-gap issue facing immigrants. Important questions are being raised in the halls of the Capitol about how to treat non-English-speaking individuals in the United States. For example, does government have a role in providing non-English-speaking people with translations of ballots, tax forms, and other government documentation? Should tax dollars go toward English instructional classes for immigrants? Should the federal government pass laws to establish English as the official national language, prohibiting any government office from offering bilingual assistance to non-English-speaking individuals?

Proponents of English-only legislation believe that mandating spoken and written English in all public discourse encourages assimilation of immigrants into the mainstream culture. They stress that a bilingual society promotes divisions among ethnic groups and increases economic difficulties for illegal immigrants hoping to move from the shadows into citizenship. After all, they argue, an illegal migrant worker will not progress beyond picking strawberries in a California field if he or she does not command the fundamental tools of communication. Plus, the effects of this limitation could be cumulative and intergenerational, as his or her children will be likelier to have educational difficulties, endangering their own economic futures.

Of course, the challenge of assimilation is broader than the language an illegal immigrant speaks. But the English language is a touchstone of the illegal immigration debate because a common language is essential in the social interaction of health care, education, and tax systems. Indeed, it is basic to the democratic process of voting.

Mauro E. Mujica, chairman of U.S. English, Inc., a group advocating for English-only legislation, suggests that the "lack of an assimilation policy for immigrants to the United States is rapidly changing the successful integration ways of the past." Mujica points to his personal experience as an example. He immigrated to the United States from Chile in 1965 to attend Columbia University, and learning English was never an option for him. If he were going to succeed as a student at an American university, then speaking English was essential.

Mujica maintains that the push for a more bilingual society may discourage illegal immigrants from learning English, creating a further divide between exclusively English-speaking Americans and immigrants who speak little English or only their native language. There are many areas of the country, particularly in the Southwest, where immigrants self-segregate into Spanish-speaking communities, discouraging cultural integration within the larger society.

Mujica proposes that federal money currently spent on translation services could be better utilized: "We believe it makes far more sense to funnel the money spent on translation services to providing newcomers with the most important instrument in their life's toolbox—the knowledge of English so they can go as far as their dreams take them."

However, other English-only advocates would take all federal funds away from non-English-speaking people.

In 2006, Senator James Inhofe, a Republican from Oklahoma, added an amendment to the Comprehensive Immigration Reform Bill that would have established English as the national language. Although the immigration bill was never passed, Senator Inhofe was not deterred.

One year later, he introduced the S.I. Hayakawa Official English Language Bill (S. 1335), which states, "Unless otherwise authorized or provided by law, no person has a right, entitlement or claim to have the government of the United States or any of its officials or representatives act, communicate, perform or provide services, or provide materials in any language other than English." As of November 2007, the bill had been read and referred to the Committee on Homeland Security and Governmental Affairs, where as of February 2008 it awaited a vote.

A 2006 *New York Times* editorial criticized the Inhofe bill, suggesting a solution more commensurate with Mujica's proposal: "People who struggle with the language don't need to be told how important English fluency is in America. If Mr. Inhofe wanted to lavish federal money on English-language classes, now overwhelmed with immigrants on waiting lists, such a step would do more to advance the cause of English and assimilation than any xenophobic amendment." Indeed, it is largely a myth that immigrants are not willing to learn English. The vast majority of the immigrant population is eager to speak the mainstream language. However, instructional resources are not always readily available.

The American Civil Liberties Union (ACLU) also weighed in on Inhofe's amendment: "This country needs better access to English education for limited speakers, not a mute button on government access for millions of Americans." The ACLU also cautioned, "Some versions of the proposed English Language Amendment would void almost all state and federal laws that require the government to provide services in languages other than English. The services affected would include: health, education, and social welfare services; job training and translation assistance to crime victims and witnesses in court and administrative proceedings; voting assistance and ballots; driver's licensing exams, and AIDS-prevention education."

That being said, many Americans might be surprised to know that their tax dollars are being spent on providing translation services and the teaching of English to non-English-speakers. In the abstract, it is easy to think of better ways to allocate government dollars. But like most controversial issues, the underlying effects of Inhofe's legislation are more complicated than they appear. If the government did not pay for these translation services, the health of many immigrants could be endangered, economic disparities among non-English-speakers could worsen, democracy could be threatened by disenfranchising voters who are unable to read English-only ballots, and taxes could go unpaid because of single language forms.

It is nonetheless a delicate balance to strike between wanting immigrants' assimilation and ensuring that all people within U.S. borders are adequately provided for. Moreover, though the welfare of immigrants, illegal or not, is paramount to a sense of national pride and human decency, it is also wise to heed the warning of former president Theodore Roosevelt in 1919: "We have room for but one language in this country, and that is the English language, for we intend to see that the crucible turns our people out as Americans, of American nationality, and not as dwellers in a polyglot [multilingual] boarding house." Put another way, it is easy to foresee a United States tied into knots by a bureaucracy struggling to accommodate a multilingual society, but losing a larger national unity in the process.

Invoking Roosevelt shows that the English-only debate is not new. After the Louisiana Purchase in 1803, the United States acquired a new population of French-speaking citizens. Decades later, French-language rights were abandoned in Louisiana after the Civil War. Also, at an 1868 conference on Indian rights, it was recommended that Native Americans be provided an English-only education. These events, along with others, were designed at least in part to encourage assimilation with the force of law. It remains to be seen how the country will untangle this issue in the twenty-first century.

Although people in the United States may never come to a totally amicable solution to the problem of language, it is important to keep a sense of perspective. The United States endures despite or because of its cultural diversity. Historically described as a melting pot, the United States faces in the early 2000s the issue of illegal immigration, and many people recognize that one complication in that complex subject is the matter of language. They realize that mutual understanding depends on sharing a language and that sharing a language requires strategies for overcoming language barriers.

CHAPTER 1

Illegal Immigrants and Cultural Assimilation

Americans Are Divided Over Illegal Immigrants

Pew Research Center for the People and the Press

The Pew Research Center is an independent opinion research group that studies attitudes toward the press, politics, and public policy issues. It is highly regarded for its national surveys that measure public perceptions of major news stories and for its polls, which monitor trends in cultural, political, and social attitudes. In this introduction to a larger 2006 report on Americans' perceptions of illegal immigration, the authors point to a number of trends and divisions within the public. As a whole, the authors of the study found that Americans' opinions regarding Latino and Asian immigrants have largely improved since the 1990s and that most U.S. citizens polled do not rate illegal immigration to be among the more pressing political issues of their time. The report also reveals that the American public is in large part skeptical toward the government entities addressing this issue and is split over which policy solutions it believes will best curb illegal immigration. Not necessarily political, these divisions are typically socioeconomic, as financially struggling and less-educated Americans more often believe illegal immigrants to be a burden on society and are more likely to favor stricter policies.

Americans are increasingly concerned about immigration. A growing number believe that immigrants are a burden to the country, taking jobs and housing and creating strains on the health care system. Many people also worry about the cultural impact of the expanding number of newcomers in the U.S.

Yet the public remains largely divided in its views of the overall effect of immigration. Roughly as many believe that

Pew Research Center for the People and the Press, "America's Immigration Quandary: No Consensus On Immigration Problem Or Proposed Fixes (Introduction)," *The Pew Research Center*, March 30, 2006.

newcomers to the U.S. strengthen American society as say they threaten traditional American values, and over the longer term, positive views of Latin American immigrants, in particular, have improved dramatically.

Policy Differences

Reflecting this ambivalence, the public is split over many of the policy proposals aimed at dealing with the estimated 11.5 million–12 million unauthorized migrants in the U.S. Overall, 53% say people who are in the U.S. illegally should be required to go home, while 40% say they should be granted some kind of legal status that allows them to stay here.

But nearly half of those who believe illegal immigrants should be required to leave nonetheless say that some could stay under a temporary work program. Overall, the public divides about evenly among three main approaches for dealing with people who are in this country illegally: 32% think it should be possible for them to stay permanently; 32% believe some should be allowed to stay under a temporary worker program under the condition that they leave eventually; and 27% think that all illegal immigrants should be required to go home.

There is also a division of opinion over how to stem the flow of illegal immigrants across the Mexican border. When asked to choose among three options, roughly half of Americans (49%) say increasing the penalties for employers who hire illegal immigrants would be most effective in reducing illegal cross-border immigration, while a third prefer boosting the number of border patrol agents. Just 9% of the public says the construction of more fences along the Mexican border would be most effective.

A Marginal Issue for Most

In general, however, the issue of immigration is not a top-tier problem for most Americans. Just 4% volunteer it as the most important problem facing the country, far fewer than the number mentioning the war in Iraq, dissatisfaction with the government, terrorism, and several other issues.

Nor does immigration loom particularly large as a local community issue. The new survey by the Pew Research Center for the People & the Press and the Pew Hispanic Center, conducted Feb. 8–March 7 [2006] among 2,000 adults nationally, includes separate surveys of an additional 800 adults in each of five metropolitan areas that have experienced differing rates of immigration in recent years: Phoenix, Las Vegas, Chicago, Raleigh-Durham and Washington DC.

Immigration emerges as a dominant local concern only in Phoenix, near a major entry point for illegal immigrants, where 55% say it is a very big problem. In the four other metropolitan areas, traffic congestion rates as a bigger problem than immigration.

Positive Perceptions of Immigrants

The survey finds a number of opinions about immigrants that may well contribute to ambivalent attitudes toward immigration, especially in areas where immigrants are most numerous. First, attitudes toward both Latin American and Asian immigrants are more positive now [in 2006] than in the 1990s, even as concern over the problems associated with immigration has increased. Both groups are overwhelmingly seen as very hard working and having strong family values. Impressions of Latin American immigrants, in particular, have grown much more positive, with 80% describing them as very hard working compared with 63% nearly a decade ago.

Moreover, native-born Americans who live in areas with the highest concentration of immigrants hold more positive opinions of them. Analysis of the survey indicates that their more favorable views do not merely reflect their demographics or political composition, but suggests that exposure to and experience with immigrants results in a better impression of them. However, Americans living in areas with more immigrants rank immigration as a bigger community problem.

Job Concerns

And while there is concern about the impact of immigration on the availability of jobs, nearly two-thirds (65%) say that immigrants coming to the country mostly take jobs that Americans do not want, rather than take jobs away from Americans. In this regard, the recent influx of immigrants into such metropolitan areas as Phoenix, Las Vegas and Raleigh-Durham has not undermined the generally positive perceptions residents have of the local job market.

Yet at the same time, a sizable minority (16%) says they or a family member have lost a job to an immigrant worker. And the perception of being passed over—more common among those with less education and lower incomes—is strongly associated with negative views of immigrants and high levels of support for strong measures to deal with the problem. For example, 75% of those who say they or a family member has lost a job to an immigrant view them as a burden compared with 47% of those who do not think this has happened.

Split Over Policy Solutions

The public's divisions over illegal immigration are mirrored in views of legal immigration; 40% say the current level should be decreased, but almost the same number (37%) believe it should be kept at its present level, while 17% prefer to see it increased.

But it is illegal immigration, far more than legal immigration, that stirs public anxiety. Six-in-ten say illegal immigration represents a bigger problem than legal immigration. Just 4% say the opposite—that legal immigration is a bigger problem—though nearly a quarter (22%) says both forms of immigration are equally problematic.

Besides economic concerns, many express worries that illegal immigrants contribute to crime and increase the danger of terrorism. Yet fewer see tougher border controls, relative to employer sanctions, as the most effective way to reduce illegal immigration along the Mexican border. Even those who are most worried about the threat of terrorism associated with illegal immigration favor employer fines over border fences and more agents.

In line with these attitudes, two-thirds of the public favors the creation of a new government database for all of those eligible to work—citizens and legal immigrants alike—and a requirement that employers check this database before hiring new workers. Even more Americans support a de facto national identification card—either a Social Security card or new form of driver's license—that job applicants would be required to show before obtaining a job.

Like policymakers, the public is conflicted about what to do with immigrants who are here illegally. Beyond questions of their legal status, Americans express very different opinions about providing government services for such people—and their children. By a wide margin (67%–29%), Americans believe that illegal immigrants should be ineligible for social services provided by state and local governments. Yet by an equally lopsided margin (71%–26%), most feel that the children of illegal immigrants should be permitted to attend public schools.

The Proximity Factor

The survey finds a complex relationship between exposure to immigrants and opinions about them and the immigration problem, more generally. People who live in areas that have high concentrations of immigrants are less likely to see them as a burden to society and a threat to traditional American customs and values. However, they are more apt than others to see immigration as an important problem for their local community.

In sharp contrast, native-born Americans who live in areas with few immigrants understandably are less inclined to see immigration as a local problem. However, many more of those in areas with relatively low concentrations of foreign-born people see immigrants as a burden to the nation and as a threat to American customs. People living in areas with few immigrants have a considerably more negative opinion of Hispanics and a slightly more negative view of Asians.

In general, the survey shows broad public recognition of the increasing level of immigration in recent years. Significantly more Americans than in the 1990s think that there are "many" recent immigrants living in their communities (35% currently vs. 17% in 1997). In each of the metropolitan areas surveyed separately, with the exception of Chicago, nearly half say there are many recent immigrants in their area.

Similarly, as many as 49% nationwide say they often come in contact with people who speak little or no English, up from 28% in 1997. This experience is very common in Las Vegas and Phoenix—68% of Las Vegas residents and 66% of Phoenix residents say they often encounter people who speak little or no English. Most Americans who come in contact with people with little English say it does not bother them (61%), compared with 38% who say that it does. The balance of opinion is similar in the five metropolitan area surveys.

Political Breakdown

The American public is not particularly confident in its political leadership to deal with immigration. President [George W.] Bush and the Republicans get especially anemic [weak] grades. Only 42% have a lot or some confidence in President Bush to do the right thing with regard to the issue. The Republican Party gets a similar rating (45%).

The Democratic Party achieves an only somewhat better evaluation (53%) as do governors (54%) and local leaders (56%). Residents of the five metropolitan areas surveyed separately evaluate their political leadership on the immigration issue about the same way citizens do nationwide. The exception is Governor Janet Napolitano of Arizona and local officials in Phoenix who achieve better ratings than other governors and local leaders.

Hispanics are more critical of all political leaders than are other citizens, but especially with respect to the Republican Party. However, they give President Bush a somewhat better grade than they do the GOP ["Grand Old Party": the Republicans] (41% vs. 33%).

For the most part, partisanship has only a modest impact on attitudes toward the severity of the problems associated with immigration and possible solutions. On basic attitudes as to how to reduce illegal immigration from Mexico, roughly half of Republicans, Democrats and independents prefer tougher employer sanctions; only about one-in-ten in each group thinks the construction of more border fences would be the most effective measure. About the same number of Republicans and Democrats also say illegal immigrants in the U.S. must go home. However, it is noteworthy that while Republicans express somewhat more concern about immigration overall, a plurality favors a temporary worker program for immigrants, a position President Bush has championed.

Other Divides

Concerns about immigration, and views of what to do about it, divide the public in many different ways. Significant disagreement exists between college graduates and those who did not attend or complete college, between people who are struggling financially and those who are doing well, between liberals and conservatives, and along ethnic lines. While African Americans differ little from whites in their views about most of these issues, Latinos hold consistently more favorable views of immigrants and the impact of immigration on American society.

As a result, even when Republicans and Democrats do not differ overall, there are often deep divides within the political parties along ideological and socioeconomic lines. Generally financially struggling and less educated people hold more negative views of immigrants and favor more strict policies than do the financially secure and college graduates, and this is the case within both party coalitions.

For example, Republicans who rate their financial situation as "only fair" or "poor" are 20 points more likely than those who say they are in "excellent" or "good" shape to say immigrants are a burden on the country because they take jobs, housing and health care, and the gap between secure and insecure Democrats is comparably large. Within each party, education also plays a major factor—Democrats without a college degree are more than twice as likely to want to see legal immigration decreased compared with those who have a four-year degree.

City Surveys

In addition, the survey looked at five metropolitan areas that have experienced a significant increase in the foreign-born population. While respondents in Phoenix, Chicago, Las Vegas, Raleigh-Durham and Washington DC had similar views on some aspects of immigration and immigrants, there were also significant differences.

- Phoenix is the only metropolitan area where immigration is cited as the most important local problem.

- In Las Vegas, a majority says that immigrants from Latin America keep to themselves and do not try to fit in, the highest among the metro areas and significantly higher than the national result.

- Chicago, a historically diverse city, has seen recent population gains primarily from Hispanics. Residents of the area are generally more tolerant of immigrants and less inclined to support punitive measures for illegal immigrants.

- In Raleigh-Durham, a sizable majority believes that recent immigrants do not pay their share of taxes.

- Washington DC has a generally more welcoming view of immigrants compared with the other metropolitan areas.

The Government Should Have a Role in Encouraging Assimilation

Karin Brulliard

This 2007 article from the Washington Post *examines the role federal government has taken in promoting assimilation and looks at the future of public initiatives. Although assimilation by about the third generation of an immigrant family used to be a foregone conclusion, according to researchers, it is now more difficult for immigrants, and particularly illegal immigrants, to integrate into U.S. society. For some of the people interviewed in the piece, this means that government agencies need to become more aggressive in encouraging assimilation through English-language programs and other initiatives. Still others are worried that immigrants' lack of integration into U.S. society will have a splintering effect on American culture as a whole. While ultimately it may be the responsibility of the immigrants themselves to assimilate into U.S. society, many of those interviewed in this article believe that it is in the interest of the United States to lend a helping hand. Karin Brulliard is a* Washington Post *staff reporter who has a master's degree in Latin American Studies.*

Hernan Ruiz, a concrete finisher with a gray streak in his dark hair, shot up his hand during a recent citizenship test prep class at a sunny Silver Spring [Maryland] community center. Called on to answer a question about who elects the U.S. president, the El Salvador native carefully pronounced "electoral college," a response he might need to know for his official transformation into an American.

After 22 years in the United States, Ruiz said, he feels like one.

But he knows that not everyone sees people such as him—an immigrant who prefers to speak his mother tongue—that way. To this, he responds that the U.S. government should demand that newcomers know English—and help them learn it.

"This country was founded by immigrants. There should be a lot of cultures," Ruiz, 48, said. "But at the base is the government."

The Role of Government

Ruiz's idea lies at the heart of a question that has recently entered the national immigration debate, one some researchers say is important as new trends challenge old integration patterns: Should the government encourage assimilation?

The [George W.] Bush administration is taking steps to do that. The Task Force on New Americans, created [in 2006] by executive order, recently [as of August 2007] presented initiatives that supporters say will help immigrants "become fully American."

Among the government initiatives is a Web site to direct immigrants to information on benefits, English classes and volunteer work. Another site offers resources for English and citizenship-test teachers. More than 12,000 copies of a tool kit containing civics flashcards and a welcome guide in English and Spanish have been distributed to libraries. This fall [2007], the government has scheduled eight regional training conferences for civics and citizenship instructors. The task force is to deliver more recommendations to President Bush after convening discussions on assimilation with immigrant advocates, teachers and local officials around the nation.

Immigrants "need to come here and feel as American as the founding fathers," Emilio T. Gonzalez, director of U.S. Citizenship and Immigration Services at the Department of Homeland Security, said at a news conference announcing the efforts.

Multigenerational Process

Social scientists emphasize that assimilation has never been a first-generation process. They rely on such measurements as language, education, economic mobility, intermarriage and geographic distribution to assess assimilation—the test of which is not a loss of ethnic identity, but parity with the majority. The massive wave of immigrants a century ago made few gains, but its grandchildren were integrated.

The modern immigrant wave arrived after laws were relaxed in 1965, so evidence of its generational progress remains incomplete, said Tomas R. Jimenez, assistant sociology professor at the University of California at San Diego. But researchers say the newcomers and their offspring seem to be following the broad historical pattern, although Mexicans are progressing more slowly. English acquisition is occurring at the same or a faster rate, said Rubén G. Rumbaut, a sociology professor at the University of California at Irvine.

Although adult immigrants generally have a hard time learning English, their children are commonly bilingual. "By the third generation, it's over. English wins. Even among Mexicans in Southern California," said Rumbaut, whose research has found that more than 95 percent of third- and later-generation California Mexicans prefer to speak English at home.

Changed Equation

Still, there are indications that the assimilation equation has changed, researchers said.

Thirty percent of immigrants are here illegally, about double the rate 15 years ago [in 1992]. Illegal status limits economic mobility and public benefits. Fear of being deported—particularly as tensions boil over illegal immigration—means "you're not likely to go out and integrate much beyond what you must," said Michael Fix, co-director of the nonpartisan Migration Policy Institute's National Center on Immigrant Integration Policy.

Drawn by demand for low-skill labor, immigrants are increasingly settling in smaller cities and rural areas, and those doing so are more likely to be poor, non-English-speaking and illegal. It is unclear whether that quickens integration by forcing contact with U.S. natives at the local park or slows it because the receiving communities have little experience bringing immigrants into the fold, Fix said.

Communications and travel revolutions have enabled immigrants to keep closer ties to their homelands, perhaps creating more transnational identities. Unlike in the 1920s, when foreigners were all but prevented from immigrating to the United States, today's immigrants keep coming, and most speak one language: Spanish. That means generations can maintain contact with ancestral cultures and tongues.

And the institutions that prompted assimilation in the early 20th century—labor unions, a manufacturing economy, the military draft and political parties that once held sway in many cities—are weakened or gone, researchers say. Today's labor economy fills some, but not all, of the void.

"Historically, certain institutions have been very important in terms of bringing immigrants into American life around issues of politics, American democracy and jobs," said Gary Gerstle, a Vanderbilt University history professor. "Immersion in American culture [alone] doesn't bring you those things."

Culture Clashes

What these trends mean is unclear. Some researchers say assimilation will occur anyway; others sound alarms.

"We are dramatically less able to digest immigrants successfully and turn them into Americans" than before, said Mark Krikorian, executive director of the Center for Immigration Studies, which favors reduced immigration levels. "The consequences are a kind of balkanization" [fragmentation].

John Fonte, director of the Center for American Common Culture at the right-leaning Hudson Institute, predicts a "long-term decay" of American identity.

Fix said the trends do not indicate that the nation is on "the threshold of a culture war." But the possibility of a permanent underclass—if immigrants' descendants do not advance economically or educationally—is too great to leave to chance, especially in an economy that increasingly demands higher skills, he said.

For that reason, he and other scholars say, assimilation policy should be as much a part of the immigration debate as rules on who comes and goes—and the federal government should get far more involved. They call for a national integration office to set and measure goals and serve as a liaison for local governments and organizations that do the bulk of work with immigrants. Aggressive, professional English programs also are a key, Fix said.

Government Efforts

So is more money, Jimenez said. According to the Migration Policy Institute, the federal government spent about $2.5 billion on major initiatives directed at the nation's 35 million immigrants in fiscal 2005, most of which went to refugee and migrant worker programs. In 1986, the government gave $4 billion to states to offset costs associated with legalizing 2.8 million immigrants in 1986. The federal task force has spent $1.5 million, officials said.

"A lot of people will see any government involvement as a sort of cultural engineering. Folks on the left won't like it because of that, and folks on the right won't like it because it's spending money on immigrants," Jimenez said. "To the folks on the left, I'd say this is about creating economic opportunity. And to folks on the right, this is about securing the future of the United States."

Krikorian said the government is right to step in, but "unless we dramatically reduce the inflow of people from abroad, this kind of effort is just trying to wipe the ocean up with the sponge."

As director of the African Resources Center in the District, Abdul Kamus tries to teach immigrants the virtues of democracy. He bristled at the idea of a federal task force on assimilation. But he said organizations such as his—on which he said he has spent his retirement money—need more funding and help.

"There are not enough [English as a Second Language] classes. I would suggest to Americans, if they really want to help immigrants quote-unquote assimilate, they should teach a family English," Kamus said.

Becoming American

Assimilation patterns mean little to Mulu Zemikel, 49, even though her life fits into some of the traditional ones.

The Eritrea native immigrated more than two decades ago with no English skills. She and her husband settled in what was then an ethnic enclave for Ethiopians and Eritreans, Adams Morgan, [a Washington, D.C. neighborhood] where they opened an Eritrean restaurant that served foul, a fava bean chili, to crowds of compatriots.

Today, the enclave's population has dispersed to the suburbs. Her customers include Americans who have discovered foul, Zemikel said. Her three U.S.-born children are fully American, she said—except that they are more "disciplined." Zemikel, a U.S. citizen, picked up her fractured English from them. She uses it to communicate with the restaurant's Salvadoran and Mexican cooks.

No government program directly aided Zemikel's integration. If anything made her embrace her new country, she said, it was the diversity that worries some critics.

Americans "want all the people—black, yellow, green, Chinese," Zemikel said. "In other countries, they don't want them, like, equal."

At the Silver Spring citizenship class, Alcides Orellana quietly filled out his workbook. He is 34 and emigrated from El Salvador at 17. His conversational English is rocky, but his hobby of studying U.S. history on the Internet has made him fluent in such American mottoes as "freedom for all."

He knows few other immigrants who go to such lengths, but government assimilation projects might help, he said.

"If you live in America," Orellana said, "you have to be American."

Immigrants Are Assimilating Into American Culture

Stephen J. Trejo

Stephen J. Trejo is an associate professor of economics at the University of Texas at Austin. He has written many scholarly articles concerning the status and mobility of Mexican Americans in the U.S. labor market. In this 2006 article, Trejo delves into the debate over Mexican Americans' assimilation and takes an intergenerational view. Although he acknowledges that immigrants' assimilation is more difficult in modern times than it was in the past, he is also encouraged by the progress that Mexican Americans are making on an intergenerational time scale. From intermarriage with non-Mexican Americans to English acquisition, Trejo stresses that the road to assimilation often takes several generations but still arrives at the same destination: full integration into American society. Although there is still a troublesome education gap between Mexican Americans and their white counterparts, Trejo believes that Mexican Americans are treading a similar path toward assimilation that their European counterparts followed a century ago.

I agree with [author] Richard Rodriguez that economists have no special expertise in answering many of the most important questions raised by Mexican immigration. Indeed, economic arguments are often adopted by advocates on either side of the debate as a socially acceptable way of advancing positions that really have more to do with thorny issues of culture, race, and religion. Nonetheless, because it's what I know something about, I'm going to focus on the issue of economic assimilation. Furthermore, I'm going to take a longer-term perspective by looking past the immigrant generation to instead consider the U.S.-born descendants of Mexican immigrants.

As a self-styled "nation of immigrants," the United States takes great pride in its historical success as a "melting pot" able to absorb and unify people coming from diverse lands and cultures. At the same time, however, pride in our immigrant heritage always seems tempered by the nagging fear that the most recent arrivals are somehow different, that the latest wave of foreigners won't integrate into the mainstream of American society. Certainly, this fear was voiced when Italians and other relatively unskilled immigrants arrived in large numbers at the end of the 1800s and the beginning of the 1900s. Time has assuaged this particular fear. In terms of outcomes such as educational attainment, occupation, and earnings, the sizable differences by national origin that initially persisted among earlier European immigrants have largely disappeared among the modern-day descendants of these immigrants.

Assimilation Harder Today

Are Mexicans following the same intergenerational trajectory as European Immigrants? Many doubt it, and they can point to several factors that might slow the pace of assimilation by Mexicans today as compared to Europeans in the past. For example, consider the vast scale of current immigration flows from Mexico and other Spanish-speaking countries, the substantial (though lessening) geographic concentration of these flows within the United States, and the fact that such flows have remained sizable over a much longer period of time than did the influx from any particular European country. These features of Mexican immigration foster the growth of ethnic enclaves in the United States where Mexicans and their descendants could, if they so choose, live and work without being forced to learn English or to Americanize in other important ways.

In addition, today's economy provides fewer opportunities for unskilled workers to advance than did the economy that greeted earlier European immigrants. Around 1900, high school completion was uncommon for native-born Americans, so while many European immigrants arrived with relatively meager educations, their skill disadvantage was smaller than that faced today by Mexican immigrants who almost always lack the additional years of high school and college that have become the norm for U.S. natives. Moreover, recent decades have witnessed a large rise in earnings inequality among American workers, driven by substantial increases in the labor market payoffs to education and other indicators of skill. As a result, the skill deficit of Mexican immigrants has become even more of a liability in our modern economy that places a higher premium on knowledge and cognitive ability.

Intergenerational Success

What do we know about the socioeconomic achievement of the children, grandchildren, and more distant descendants of Mexican immigrants? In light of the reasons for pessimism listed above, U.S.-born Mexican Americans have done surprisingly well, though certainly areas of serious concern remain. Like Europeans in the past, Mexicans enjoy ample intergenerational progress between first-generation immigrants and their second-generation children. Relative to their parents, the U.S.-born second generation experiences dramatic increases in English proficiency, educational attainment, and earnings. From this generational perspective, the lightning-rod issue of language—in terms of both English acquisition and Spanish preservation—loses all its spark. By the time they are teens, second-generation Mexican Americans overwhelmingly prefer to speak English rather than Spanish, and by the third generation most Mexican Americans no longer speak Spanish at all.

In general, the labor market opportunities available to U.S.-born Mexican Americans are similar to those afforded non-Hispanic whites with identical skills. On average, the employment and earnings of Mexican Americans are close to the outcomes of Anglos who are the same age and have the same schooling. In contrast, the situation for African-American men is very different, with large and persistent black-white gaps in employment rates and earnings even after accounting for education and other measurable skill characteristics. Consequently, the potential role of other factors—such as discrimination, family background, or neighborhood—in explaining economic disadvantage is smaller for Mexican Americans than for African Americans. Even outside of the labor market context, Mexicans seem to be faring better than blacks. On two important indicators of socially risky behavior, male incarceration and unwed motherhood, the rates for U.S.-born Mexican Americans exceed those of Anglos but do not approach the very high rates of African Americans.

Education Gap

There is one crucial area, however, where Mexican Americans lag behind both whites and blacks: education. This problem is well-known, although popular accounts often greatly exaggerate its magnitude by not distinguishing Mexican immigrants from U.S.-born Mexican Americans. Nonetheless, high school dropout is disturbingly prevalent for U.S.-born Mexicans, even for those in the third generation and beyond (i.e., for the U.S.-born grandchildren and later descendants of Mexican immigrants). Inevitably, college attendance and completion rates are also much lower for Mexican Americans. Because the educational disadvantage of this group largely explains their below-average earnings, finding a way to eliminate the schooling gap would go a long way toward bridging the economic divide that remains between Mexican Americans and the Anglo majority. As Rodriguez notes, the limited educational success of U.S.-born Mexicans may reflect cultural pressures to subordinate personal achievement for the sake of family unity, a social dynamic that Rodriguez aptly describes as the struggle between competing pronouns "I" and "we". Surely, however, some other immigrant groups (e.g., Italians) faced a similar dynamic and still were able to integrate fully into American society, so perhaps we can expect that ultimately the same thing will occur for Mexicans.

Intermarriage

Frequent intermarriage is one of the strongest signals of social assimilation by an ethnic group. After a few generations in the United States, so much intermarriage had taken place among the descendants of earlier European immigrants that most white Americans could choose among multiple ancestries or ethnic identities. For such individuals, ethnicity has become subjective, situational, and largely symbolic, and the social boundaries between these ethnic groups have been almost completely erased.

In this context, it is encouraging to note that intermarriage is widespread among Mexican Americans. More than a third of married, U.S.-born Mexicans have non-Mexican spouses, with the overwhelming majority of these non-Mexican spouses being U.S.-born, non-Hispanic whites. Because it takes two Mexican-origin spouses to create an endogamous Mexican marriage, whereas a Mexican intermarriage requires only one Mexican-origin spouse, the observed rate of intermarriage implies that almost half of Mexican-American marriages involve a non-Mexican spouse.

Co-author [and economics professor] Brian Duncan and I have begun to study how Mexican intermarriage influences the ethnic identification of the children produced by these marriages. Not surprisingly, virtually all children with two Mexican-origin parents are identified as Mexican in Census data, but about 30 percent of the children of intermarried Mexican Americans are not identified as Mexican. As this dynamic plays out across generations, it is likely that an increasingly small fraction of the descendants of Mexican immigrants continue to identify themselves as Mexican. Moreover, this process of ethnic leakage is highly selective, because Mexican Americans who intermarry tend to have much higher education and earnings than Mexican Americans who do not intermarry. Consequently, available data for third- and higher-generation Mexicans, who usually can only be identified by their subjective responses to questions about Hispanic ethnicity, probably understate the socioeconomic attainment of this population. In effect, through the selective nature of intermarriage and ethnic identification, some of the most successful descendants of Mexican immigrants assimilate to such an extent that they fade from empirical observation. Unfortunately, although the direction of this measurement bias seems clear, we don't yet have a good idea of its magnitude.

On the Right Path

Overall, my reading of the evidence is that Mexican Americans are not too far off the path of intergenerational assimilation traveled by previous waves of European immigrants. During their first few generations in the United States, Mexican-American families experience substantial economic and social mobility, and their actual progress is probably even greater than what we see in available data. The relatively slow rate of educational improvement is a critical problem, however, especially because the schooling deficit of Mexican Americans is the major obstacle to their economic integration. Another potential concern is that many Mexicans enter the United States as illegal immigrants. Rodriguez makes the compelling point that growing up in an undocumented household could have profound effects on the children of Mexican immigrants, but unfortunately I'm not aware of any research on the intergenerational impact of illegal immigration. Despite these concerns, I agree with the broad conclusion reached by historian Joel Perlmann, whose book *Italians Then, Mexicans Now* carefully compares the intergenerational mobility experienced by low-skill European immigrants arriving in the United States around 1900 with that experienced by modern-day Mexicans. Perlmann suggests that "Mexican economic assimilation may take more time—four or five generations rather than three or four." If Perlmann is right, then the long-term integration of Mexican Americans may not turn out all that differently from the success stories often recounted for previous waves of U.S. immigration.

Immigrants Are Not Assimilating Into American Culture

David Frum

David Frum is a columnist and a resident fellow at the American Enterprise Institute, a conservative think tank. A Harvard Law School graduate, Frum is also a former special assistant for economic speechwriting to President George W. Bush. *In this 2006 article from* National Review, *Frum highlights education and wage gaps that exist between Mexican immigrants and their white counterparts. He argues that these disparities in educational accomplishments and earnings persist well into the second and third generations, creating a permanent American underclass. Speculating on the future, Frum envisions a United States that is more hostile to conservative principles of limited government and reduced social programs, and more inclined toward a renewal of the kind of class warfare that he believes pervaded the country's past.*

Mexican immigrants like it in America. They are much more likely than other immigrants to rate life in the United States as superior to life in the country where they were born, according to survey research by [nonpartisan research organization] Public Agenda in 2003. They come to work: They are much less likely than other immigrants to cite political freedom as the reason for their migration. They show near zero interest in radical politics: Aside from a few loony college professors, the mystic cause of reuniting the southwestern United States to Mexico seems to excite almost nobody. They crossed the desert to escape Mexico, not to rejoin it. Whatever is going on, it isn't a Reconquista [reconquest].

So . . . good news, right? Assimilation is working? Not exactly. Mexican immigrants may like America, but they are having serious trouble joining it. Well into the second and third generations after arrival, they remain much poorer than other Americans—with unsettling long-term political and economic consequences for the United States.

Education Problems

Only 7 percent of Mexican immigrants arrive in the United States able to speak English. Few possess much formal education. These deficiencies shunt them into low-wage sectors of the economy. The economist George Borjas calculates that Mexican Americans earn almost 40 percent less than American-born workers with American-born parents. Low wages hold Mexican Americans in poverty—and the evidence suggests that their families will remain poor into the second and third generations.

Lacking English and formal education themselves, Mexican-American immigrants do not seem to attach much importance to their children's acquiring [it] either. While 82 percent of immigrants from Europe feel that all immigrants should be expected to learn English, and even 61 percent of non-Mexican Latinos agree, only a bare majority of Mexican immigrants, 54 percent, think English essential, again according to the Public Agenda survey. While 67 percent of non-Mexican immigrants think that public-school classes should be taught exclusively in English, only 51 percent of Mexicans think so.

Perhaps unsurprisingly, the children of these migrants do not flourish in school. A Manhattan Institute study of the high-school class of 1998 found that only 54 percent of Hispanic students graduated with their class, as compared with nearly 80 percent of their white counterparts. These dropouts may later return to school or earn a high-school equivalency certificate. But they will have difficulty catching up to their classmates who finished on time. And of course the children of high-school dropouts are more likely to drop out in their turn.

Wage Gap

Borjas points out that the differences in earnings between U.S. immigrant groups and the native population persist from generation to generation. Experience would suggest that if Mexican immigrants earn 40 percent less than natives, their children will earn 20 percent less, their grandchildren 10 percent less, and so on. That's not a reassuring estimate, but the reality may well be even worse. The "experience" Borjas cites is that of immigrant families settling in the United States in the 1930s, '40s, and '50s: the golden age of blue-collar America. Even if they did not speak much English, even if they did not possess much formal education, they could find work in a factory or on a dock that paid better relative to other sectors of the economy, and offered higher inflation-adjusted wages, than the same jobs today. Post-1970 America has become a much tougher environment for those without higher education. In 1970, a 30-year-old man with a college degree earned a little more than twice as much as his counterpart with a high-school diploma. By 1990, he earned three times as much. Today, the disparity gapes wider still.

The Center for Immigration Studies has found considerable evidence that today's immigrants do considerably worse than previous immigrants, decades after arrival. In 1970, only 25.7 percent of immigrants who had lived in the United States for ten to twenty years were poor, compared with 35.1 percent of natives. By 2000, 41.4 percent of long-settled immigrants were poor, as compared with 28.8 percent of natives.

Emerging Subclass

Behind all these numbers is an emerging social reality. The immigration policies of the past two decades have imported into the United States a large population that will remain ill educated, incompletely fluent in English, and significantly poorer than the rest of the country well into the 2030s and 2040s. And President Bush's proposal to settle this population permanently—and to increase the flow of new migrants—will make the problems bigger, deeper, and more intractable.

It's troubling to turn on the television and see thousands of illegal immigrants marching behind the Mexican flag, chanting slogans that denounce America's right to control its borders. But I'd worry a lot less about the Republic of Aztlan [a Mexican separatist movement] than about a future in which the American economy rests on a linguistically distinct subclass of ill-educated low-wage workers.

Looking Into the Future

Imagine America in 2031. That's the not-so-distant future: It's a date as far ahead of us as Ronald Reagan's first inauguration is behind us. Suppose the Bush immigration plan of 2006 or something like it has been enacted. Illegal aliens have been legalized; family-reunification and guest-worker programs continue to bring millions of Mexicans and Central Americans north.

In 2031, daily life for you and your children (if I may make a demographic assumption about you, reader) probably proceeds more or less as it does today. The roads are more crowded, real estate and gasoline probably more expensive, taxes higher, and government services worse. On the other hand, many onetime luxuries have steadily declined in price. Domestic-cleaning services like Merry Maids have proliferated, as have in-home childcare and eldercare, gardening services, prepared-meal services, and car detailing. Like Alicia Silverstone in *Clueless*, you have little need to know how to parallel park—everywhere you want to go, they have valet. In short: The southern-California lifestyle has spread throughout the country. But what of the migrants whose labor sustains your pleasantly seigniorial [lordlike] life?

How do they feel about their relative poverty—a poverty cushioned but not significantly ameliorated by the food stamps, Earned Income Tax Credits, housing subsidies, and Medicaid benefits for which they are now eligible? At first, perhaps, they didn't complain much. Life in the United States represented a huge improvement over life in Mexico or Central America. First-generation migrants worked too hard, felt too insecure, and trusted government too little to agitate for a better deal. But what of their American-born but ill-educated and low-wage children?

They have the vote. They have expectations of a better life. Will they not find politicians ready to mobilize them for a new era of populist redistributionism—a redistributionism made more powerful and more exciting by the ethnic and linguistic differences between haves and have-nots?

Political Shifting

Certainly that is the future left-wing Democrats expect. Immigration reformers often express wonder that the political Left has welcomed an immigration whose main effect is to lower the wages of less-skilled workers, especially black men. But maybe the Left is playing a longer game here—where the short-term depression of living standards for working people becomes a necessary price to pay to reignite the radical economic movements that inflamed the United States from 1870 to 1940.

Americans have become so used to political and economic stability that they have forgotten that their country was once disgraced by the most violent and bloody labor conflicts on earth. These conflicts were often intensified by the ethnic differences between strikers and the American population at large—differences that exerted a follow-on effect in electoral politics. As [conservative author] Michael Barone observes in *Our Country*, his magisterial [masterly] history of 20th-century American politics, outside the South the division between support for and opposition to Franklin Delano Roosevelt's New Deal was grounded on ethnicity as much as social class, with old-stock Americans against and immigrants and the children of immigrants in favor.

Politicians like Los Angeles mayor Antonio Villaraigosa plainly hope that the trick can be repeated in this new century. As [liberal columnist] Harold Meyerson wrote in *The American Prospect*, the "Latinoization [of California] has also transformed California's fiscal politics." The state that led the tax-rebellion movement in the late 1970s and fed the national conservative political resurgence passed "a massive $9.2-billion school bond measure and a $2-billion initiative for parks and open-space preservation" in 1998, and reduced the power of anti-tax voters to veto local-government bond measures. "With the uptick in Latino voting . . . the gap between the voting public and the people who need public services began to narrow."

Many conservative immigration advocates insist that Villaraigosa and Meyerson have it wrong—that the migrants and their children and grandchildren will be socially conservative and politically quiescent. It's worth noting, though, that Republican political professionals are ceasing to believe this: That's why so many of them, from [former Bush political consultant] Karl Rove on down, now emphasize guest-worker programs as a way to benefit from immigrant labor without having to face the consequences of immigrant votes.

Anticipating Class Warfare

But as the French and Germans have discovered, there is nothing less temporary than a temporary worker. The migrants will settle, will take up their political rights—and will use those rights to advance their interests: interests that may sharply differ from those of more-established inhabitants.

For more than half a century, American society has been divided along lines of race. The most polarizing issues—busing, affirmative action, welfare, crime—have explicitly or implicitly involved race. Race has exerted so strong an influence that when new grievances came along—the rights of women, of the disabled, of gays—the grievance-bearers unselfconsciously squeezed and shoved their demands into the forms left behind by the civil-rights battles of 30, 40, and 50 years before. . . .

Race analogies so mesmerize us that we unthinkingly assume that the challenges presented by immigration must fit into this ancient envelope. It's almost impossible for us to imagine anything else—least of all something so antiquated, so remote as conflicts along the lines of class.

But everything old becomes new again. And it may well be that the greatest threat from today's immigration is not that the United States will be racially balkanized [fragmented], but that it will relive a past in which classes invoked ethnic solidarity in a struggle over wealth and power. The danger is not that immigrants won't "Americanize." They will. The danger is that they will reintroduce America to an authentically American history that once seemed long and well forgotten.

Illegal Immigrants Are Dangerous for America

R. Cort Kirkwood

R. Cort Kirkwood is managing editor of the Daily News-Record *of Harrisonburg, Virginia, and a contributor to many scholarly journals, including the conservative magazine the* New American, *which advocates for limited government. In this 2007 article, Kirkwood proposes that an illegal immigrant crime wave is overtaking the United States. Weaving individual cases with crime statistics to illustrate his point, the author implicates illegal immigrants in the robbing, raping, and murdering of Americans. He also seems to suggest that there is a cultural indifference toward the crime of rape among Mexicans. Kirkwood finds fault with U.S. governmental agencies and states that too many of these criminals are going free due to lenient immigration policies enacted by legislators. Until Americans and their politicians demand stricter enforcement of immigration laws, Kirkwood concludes, a more dangerous future for U.S. citizens awaits.*

On June 5, [2006] nine-year-old Jordin Paulder, a towheaded boy with "chubby cheeks," as the newspapers described him, was playing in the parking lot of the Chastain Apartments in Sandy Springs, Georgia, part of metro Atlanta. Jordin saw a car go by and called out to the occupants. The car had a bum tire, the lad shouted. The car stopped, and Santos Benigno Cabrera Borjas emerged, wielding a hatchet. He twice smashed Jordin in the face between the nose and forehead. The second blow buried the hatchet, which paramedics feared removing en route to the hospital. Jordin died. When police cornered Borjas as paramedics worked on Jordin, the ax-murderer tossed a rimmed tire at an officer, breaking his arm. Borjas rushed the cop, who shot him dead.

In New York on November 1, [2006] actress Adrienne Shelly died in her apartment in New York City. Shelly was found hanged by a bedsheet on a shower curtain rod, an apparent suicide. But the 40-year-old wife and mother didn't hang herself. Diego Pillco, who was renovating an apartment in Shelly's building, did the deed. He punched the woman and knocked her out when she complained about the noise. Fearing she was dead, he staged the elaborate ruse.

Borjas and Pillco have something in common. They are illegal aliens, from Honduras and Ecuador, just two of the hundreds of thousands brutalizing Americans in a crime wave of unfathomable proportions. They are robbing Americans. They are raping Americans. They are murdering Americans.

Crime Data

The crime data show that illegal aliens have unleashed a reign of terror that would have been considered an act of war 75 years ago. Consider these alarming facts: in 2003, according to the Government Accountability Office [GAO], illegal aliens composed 27 percent of the federal prison population. The majority of these, 63 percent, were Mexicans. Some 267,000 illegal aliens were jailed in federal, state, and local facilities that year. And, immigration writer Ed Rubenstein observed, while illegal aliens were an estimated 7.2 percent of the population in 2003, 12.9 percent of them were in jail or prison. In Los Angeles in 2004, 95 percent of the outstanding warrants for murder named illegal aliens.

Yet the federal government, entrusted with the responsibility to defend our country from invasion, does next to nothing. The [George W.] Bush administration gibbles and gabbles about secure borders while illegal aliens merrily inflict their mayhem. Granted, in June [2006], the federal government conducted "Operation Return to Sender," a nationwide sweep that netted 2,100 illegals (.018 percent of them, assuming 12 million total), including 367 gang bangers nationwide and three-dozen child molesters roaming free in Orange County, California. And in White Plains, New York, in December [2006], the feds arrested six illegal-alien sex offenders, some of whom were registered, on "routine visits" to the probation office. Illegal aliens are registered and make "routine visits" to the probation office? Clearly, the rest have nothing to fear. The reason? A lethal combination of federal inertia, partly due to the president's adamant refusal to deal with the problem, and state, local, and municipal "sanctuary policies" aimed at placating the Hispanic communities.

Paulder and Shelly are among the thousands of Americans who would be alive if the authorities stopped illegal immigration. Government officials frankly confess their lassitude [laxity]. Federal bureaucrats can't even keep track of their own immigrant files, and lost some 110,000 of them, the Associated Press reported in November [2006]. Of course, 30,000 citizenship applications that lacked documentation sailed through the system anyway.

Bad as that is, the crime data on illegal aliens reveal what the federal government's incompetence means. In April 2005, the GAO studied the 55,322 illegal aliens in federal prisons during 2003. The frightening facts? Those 55,322 illegal aliens were arrested 459,614 times, or eight times each. They committed some 700,000 crimes, 13 each. Thirty-six percent of them were arrested at least five times. Moreover, as Rubenstein notes, the number of illegal aliens locked in federal, state and local jails grew from 9,000 illegal aliens in 1980 to 267,000 in 2003.

Sex Crimes

Even worse, Deborah Schurman Kauflin, who heads the Violent Crimes Institute, which studied illegal aliens and crime, discovered that a disproportionate share of illegal aliens are dangerous sex fiends.

At her website, Kauflin presents her analysis of 1,500 illegal-alien cases covering nearly eight years. Most of the criminals were gathered in states with the highest number of illegals: California, Texas, Arizona, New Jersey, New York, and Florida. She uncovered a tsunami of drunk driving, robbery, child molestation, rape, and murder, including serial murders and brutal gang rapes.

Frighteningly, she reported, sex offenders represent 2 percent of illegal aliens. Assuming a population of 12 million illegals, some 240,000 illegal-alien sex criminals are now in the United States. That, in turn, "translates to 93 sex offenders and 12 serial sex offenders coming across U.S. borders illegally per day." This might be one reason Operation Return to Sender targeted illegal-alien sex criminals, and why the feds have arrested 100 sex fiends in White Plains [New York] since 2003. At any rate, Kauflin's 1,500 offenders victimized 5,999 people, about four victims each. Of those studied, 525, or 35 percent, were child molestations, 358, or 24 percent, were rapes, and 617, or 41 percent, were sexual homicides and serial murders. Illegal aliens, she calculated, victimized nearly 1 million people over the 88 months of crime data she studied.

The data are even more detailed, but you get the picture. In another article, Kauflin recounts the grisly, appalling crimes illegal aliens committed. An illegal immigrant named Maximiliano Esparza "raped and sodomized two nuns and used their rosary beads to control them during the attack. The Sisters were beaten, raped, sodomized, and finally, Esparza used her own rosary beads to strangle Sister Helen Lynn Chaska to death." Esparza, who pickled his liver [got drunk] at a strip joint before the sacrilegious attack, was a career criminal deported once before. The Border Patrol nabbed him again, but released him. Meanwhile, Kauflin observed, television drama treats us to illegal aliens attacked by Americans.

Rape Cases

These illegal-alien sex criminals are mostly Mexican. As those concerned about what immigrants mean for American culture have observed, foreigners bring their culture and customs with them. One of those beliefs, Kauflin reports, is the Mexican "concept of rapto," meaning the abduction of a woman or girl to rape her. In 2002, the *Washington Post* published a long piece backing Kauflin's opinion that rapto is "socially accept-able" in Mexico. The piece also backed her bold charge of mi-sogyny among Mexican men.

One Oaxacan legislator called rapto "romantic," which is no surprise in a country where stealing cattle, the *Post* re-ported, is more serious than rape.

"Many [Mexican] states," the paper revealed, "require that if a 12-year-old girl wants to accuse an adult man of statutory rape, she must first prove she is 'chaste and pure.'" Nineteen states simply drop statutory rape charges "if the rapist agrees to marry his victim." Outraged women's and human rights groups were trying to change Mexican law when the *Post*'s ar-ticle appeared, but whatever their success in Mexico, rapto has arrived in America. Two of the sex fiends in White Plains raped 14-year-old girls, and immigrant attacks on women and girls, including sadistic gang rapes, are rising.

One example occurred on December 19, 2002, in New York, when Victor Cruz, Armando Juvenal, Jose Hernandez, and Carlos Rodriguez, all illegal aliens, joined as many as five other men in raping a 42-year-old woman for three hours near Shea Stadium. Three of the four illegals were violent criminals but were not deported. In a letter to the court, the victim wrote that the rapists attacked her like "a pack of wild wolves." Similar examples of beastly gang rapes, some involv-ing more than a dozen men, are legion.

While many illegal-alien criminals are run-of-the-mill murderers and rapists, if such a creature exists, some of them are serial rapists and killers. The annals of illegal-alien crime, as the *New American* reported in its August 7, 2006, issue, in-clude the recently executed "Railroad Killer," Angel Maturino Resendiz. Between 1986 and 1999, he butchered at least 15 people across six states, eight in Texas and others in Kentucky and Georgia. He murdered a pastor and his wife with a sledgehammer in 1999, pulverizing the woman's face before he raped her.

Sanctuary

The bloody thread running through Kauflin's reports and other data is that many illegal aliens are caught for minor crimes and released . . . but not deported. As the *Los Angeles Times* reported about Operation Return to Sender, "most of those arrested in the nationwide sweep . . . served time in county jails. . . . But instead of being deported, they were released." If deported, illegals often return to the United States. "Nearly 63% [of the criminals Kauflin studied] had been deported on another offense prior to the sex crime. There was an average of 3 years of committing crimes such as DUI [driving under the influence], assaults or drug related offenses prior to being apprehended for a sexual offense," meaning their crimes escalated each time they were caught. The crimes Kauflin documents are so horrendous one wonders how the government erred and failed to deport the criminal illegals.

Most Americans would be shocked, or perhaps they wouldn't, to learn that federal, state, and local governments, far from making mistakes, instead refuse to deport illegal aliens. Some federal immigration officials candidly admit they are not interested in "administrative" cases, meaning those merely involving illegal immigration. The feds are interested in "other crimes." But at the state level, where such "other crimes" are committed, a different worm is eating the apple of American sovereignty. Heather McDonald, writing in *City Journal*, a publication of the Manhattan Institute, explains it in one word: sanctuary.

Many cities such as Los Angeles and New York refuse to notify federal authorities when local police apprehend criminals they know are illegal aliens. And generally, it appears, it isn't police who suggest and approve the policies. It's politicians.

Going Free

In Los Angeles, McDonald wrote, police [LAPD] can't jail dangerous gang members, despite their violent criminal records and felonious re-entry into the country, because they would violate the police department's rule against enforcing immigration laws. That rule "mirrors bans in immigrant-saturated cities . . . from New York and Chicago to San Diego, Austin, and Houston. These 'sanctuary policies' generally prohibit city employees, including the cops, from reporting immigration violations to federal authorities."

The cops, McDonald reported, are at wits' end: "We can't even talk about it," a "frustrated LAPD captain" told McDonald. "People are afraid of a backlash from Hispanics." Sighed another, "I would get a firestorm of criticism if I talked about [enforcing the immigration law against illegals]."

The consequences of this dereliction of duty are obvious, as Kauflin's report shows, but McDonald added even more examples of what not deporting illegal aliens means for law-abiding Americans. In 2004, "in Los Angeles, 95 percent of all outstanding warrants for homicide (which total 1,200 to 1,500) target illegal aliens. Up to two-thirds of all fugitive felony warrants (17,000) are for illegal aliens." In 1995, a study showed that a gang in southern California boasted 20,000 members, 60 percent of whom were illegal aliens.

Unsurprisingly, public officials defend these sanctuary policies because they believe (or say they do) that illegal-alien victims who do not fear deportation will help police, and for the insane reason that "they encourage illegals to take advantage of city services like health care and education (to whose maintenance few illegals have contributed a single tax dollar, of course)." Sanctuary may encourage more illegal aliens to jump on the welfare dole, but it hasn't curbed the crime wave. As McDonald wrote, "no one has ever suggested not enforcing drug laws, say, for fear of intimidating drug-using crime victims." In truth, McDonald reported, sheer numbers energize sanctuary policies. Politicians are afraid of the "backlash" from immigrant groups and their vociferous supporters.

Chillingly, a top presidential contender for 2008, [Rudolph] Giuliani, created a sanctuary policy and sued the federal government "all the way to the U.S. Supreme Court" over a federal law, passed in 1996, requiring cities to cooperate with federal immigration authorities. In a sequence of events so eerie it sounds fictive, six days before terrorist illegal immigrants flattened the twin towers on 9/11 and set the Pentagon ablaze, Giuliani's "handpicked charter-revision committee ruled that New York could still require that its employees keep immigration information confidential to preserve trust between immigrants and government." Pandering to illegal immigrants and their supporters, Giuliani said the federal law was a tool to "terrorize people."

Despite 9/11 and losing in court, McDonald wrote, "New York conveniently forgot the 1996 federal ban" until the flagitious [villainous] gang rape at Shea Stadium. Though three of the illegal immigrants in that case had lengthy rap sheets for violent crimes, the city "never notified the INS [Immigration and Naturalization Service]."

Bleak Future

This compendium of mayhem and murder by illegal aliens does not count the carnage on the nation's highways inflicted by drunk-driving illegal aliens. These stories are too numerous to recount here, but a quick Google search will divulge countless deaths and maimings by illegal aliens hurtling down the highways on a tankful of gas and snootful of booze. As with their other categories of crime, cases abound where illegal aliens have been caught driving drunk, then released to kill.

A particularly poignant example hit the newspapers the day after Thanksgiving [2006]. For the families of Brian Mathews, 21, of Columbia, Maryland, and Jennifer Bower, 24, of Montgomery Village, it was truly Black Friday. Eduardo Raul Morales-Soriano, 25, an illegal Mexican, killed the pair on Thanksgiving night, prosecutors allege, when he slammed his Nissan Sentra into Bower's Toyota Corolla at a red light. Mathews and Bower were on their second date.

Morales-Soriano was polluted, police allege, with four times the legal limit of alcohol. Before that fatal day, the *Baltimore Sun* disclosed, police collared him three times, the most significant being a wreck in February [2006]. Police allege he reeked of alcohol. Although he refused a Breathalyzer test, his license was not suspended, as the law requires. The charges were dropped. In July [2006], the paper reported, police nailed him for driving the wrong way on a one-way street, speeding and negligent driving. The court exonerated him. In September, before the wreck that killed Mathews and Bower, he was convicted of driving on unsafe tires. For the third time, he was not deported.

Brian Mathews, a lance corporal in the Marine Corps who survived duty in Iraq, never knew what hit him. Neither did Jordin Paulder or Adrienne Shelly, or many others who died at the hands of illegal aliens. Their demises are tragic not just for what their families and communities lost, but for what they reveal about American officialdom, from the anti-American elites in Washington to the vacillating, tremulous elites in cities and counties. They will not act. They fear an "immigrant backlash."

Until they fear an American backlash, a backlash from the Paulders and Shellys and other victims, illegal aliens will continue to rob, rape, and kill.

CHAPTER 2

The Effects of Illegal Immigration on the American Economy

Immigrants Hurt the U.S. Economy

Steven Malanga

Steve Malanga is senior editor of City Journal *and a senior fellow at the conservative Manhattan Institute. He writes about the intersection of urban economies, business communities, and public policy. In this 2006 article, Malanga proposes that illegal immigrants are a burden on the U.S. economy. The author contends that by relying more on social programs than native-born workers and taking low-skilled jobs that stifle modernization and growth, illegal immigrants represent an enormous cost for U.S. taxpayers. Malanga adds that weak assimilation on behalf of mostly Mexican immigrants, compared with earlier immigrants to the United States, makes them less likely to carve out a productive niche in U.S. society. He concludes by advocating for stricter legislative controls on immigration so that the United States might curb this growing economic threat.*

The day after Librado Velasquez arrived on [New York's] Staten Island after a long, surreptitious journey from his Chiapas, Mexico, home, he headed out to a street corner to wait with other illegal immigrants looking for work. Velasquez, who had supported his wife, seven kids, and his in-laws as a *campesino*, or peasant farmer, until a 1998 hurricane devastated his farm, eventually got work, off the books, loading trucks at a small New Jersey factory, which hired illegals for jobs that required few special skills. The arrangement suited both, until a work injury sent Velasquez to the local emergency room, where federal law required that he be treated, though he could not afford to pay for his care. After five operations, he is now permanently disabled and has remained in the United States to pursue compensation claims.

"I do not have the use of my leg without walking with a cane, and I do not have strength in my arm in order to lift things," Velasquez said through an interpreter at New York City Council hearings. "I have no other way to live except if I receive some other type of compensation. I need help, and I thought maybe my son could come and work here and support me here in the United States."

Velasquez's story illustrates some of the fault lines in the nation's current, highly charged, debate on immigration. Since the mid-1960s, America has welcomed nearly 30 million legal immigrants and received perhaps another 15 million illegals, numbers unprecedented in our history. These immigrants have picked our fruit, cleaned our homes, cut our grass, worked in our factories, and washed our cars. But they have also crowded into our hospital emergency rooms, schools, and government-subsidized aid programs, sparking a fierce debate about their contributions to our society and the costs they impose on it.

Costing the U.S. Economy

Advocates of open immigration argue that welcoming the Librado Velasquezes of the world is essential for our American economy: our businesses need workers like him, because we have a shortage of people willing to do low-wage work. Moreover, the free movement of labor in a global economy pays off for the United States, because immigrants bring skills and capital that expand our economy and offset immigration's costs. Like tax cuts, supporters argue, immigration pays for itself.

But the tale of Librado Velasquez helps show why supporters are wrong about today's immigration, as many Americans sense and so much research has demonstrated. America does not have a vast labor shortage that requires waves of low-wage immigrants to alleviate; in fact, unemployment among unskilled workers is high—about 30 percent. Moreover, many of the unskilled, uneducated workers now journeying here labor, like Velasquez, in shrinking industries, where they force out native workers, and many others work in industries where the availability of cheap workers has led businesses to suspend investment in new technologies that would make them less labor-intensive.

Yet while these workers add little to our economy, they come at great cost, because they are not economic abstractions but human beings, with their own culture and ideas— often at odds with our own. Increasing numbers of them arrive with little education and none of the skills necessary to succeed in a modern economy. Many may wind up stuck on our lowest economic rungs, where they will rely on something that immigrants of other generations didn't have: a vast U.S. welfare and social-services apparatus that has enormously amplified the cost of immigration. Just as welfare reform and other policies are helping to shrink America's underclass by weaning people off such social programs, we are importing a new, foreign-born underclass. As famed free-market economist Milton Friedman puts it: "It's just obvious that you can't have free immigration and a welfare state."

Immigration can only pay off again for America if we reshape our policy, organizing it around what's good for the economy by welcoming workers we truly need and excluding those who, because they have so little to offer, are likely to cost us more than they contribute, and who will struggle for years to find their place here. . . .

Low-Skilled Workers

The flood of immigrants, both legal and illegal, from countries with poor, ill-educated populations, has yielded a mismatch between today's immigrants and the American economy and has left many workers poorly positioned to succeed for the long term. Unlike the immigrants of 100 years ago, whose skills reflected or surpassed those of the native workforce at the time, many of today's arrivals, particularly the more than half who now come from Central and South America, are farmworkers in their home countries who come here with little education or even basic training in blue-collar occupations like carpentry or machinery. (A century ago, farmworkers made up 35 percent of the U.S. labor force, compared with the under 2 percent who produce a surplus of food today.) Nearly two-thirds of Mexican immigrants, for instance, are high school dropouts, and most wind up doing either unskilled factory work or small-scale construction projects, or they work in service industries, where they compete for entry-level jobs against one another, against the adult children of other immigrants, and against native-born high school dropouts. Of the 15 industries employing the greatest percentage of foreign-born workers, half are low-wage service industries, including gardening, domestic household work, car washes, shoe repair, and janitorial work. To take one stark example: whereas 100 years ago, immigrants were half as likely as native-born workers to be employed in household service, today immigrants account for 27 percent of all domestic workers in the United States.

Native Workers Suffer

Although open-borders advocates say that these workers are simply taking jobs Americans don't want, studies show that the immigrants drive down wages of native-born workers and squeeze them out of certain industries. Harvard economists George Borjas and Lawrence Katz, for instance, estimate that low-wage immigration cuts the wages for the average native-born high school dropout by some 8 percent, or more than $1,200 a year. Other economists find that the new workers also push down wages significantly for immigrants already here and native-born Hispanics.

Consequently, as the waves of immigration continue, the sheer number of those competing for low-skilled service jobs makes economic progress difficult. A study of the impact of immigration on New York City's restaurant business, for instance, found that 60 percent of immigrant workers do not receive regular raises, while 70 percent had never been promoted. One Mexican dishwasher aptly captured the downward pressure that all these arriving workers put on wages by telling the study's authors about his frustrating search for a 50-cent raise after working for $6.50 an hour: "I visited a few restaurants asking for $7 an hour, but they only offered me $5.50 or $6," he said. "I had to beg [for a job]."

Similarly, immigration is also pushing some native-born workers out of jobs, as Kenyon College economists showed in the California nail-salon workforce. Over a 16-year period starting in the late 1980s, some 35,600 mostly Vietnamese immigrant women flooded into the industry, a mass migration that equaled the total number of jobs in the industry before the immigrants arrived. Though the new workers created a labor surplus that led to lower prices, new services, and somewhat more demand, the economists estimate that as a result, 10,000 native-born workers either left the industry or never bothered entering it.

Slowing Modernization

In many American industries, waves of low-wage workers have also retarded investments that might lead to modernization and efficiency. Farming, which employs a million immigrant laborers in California alone, is the prime case in point. Faced with a labor shortage in the early 1960s, when President Kennedy ended a 22-year-old guest-worker program that allowed 45,000 Mexican farmhands to cross over the border and harvest 2.2 million tons of California tomatoes for processed foods, farmers complained but swiftly automated, adopting a mechanical tomato-picking technology created more than a decade earlier. Today, just 5,000 better-paid workers—one-ninth the original workforce—harvest 12 million tons of tomatoes using the machines.

The savings prompted by low-wage migrants may even be minimal in crops not easily mechanized. Agricultural economists Wallace Huffman and Alan McCunn of Iowa State University have estimated that without illegal workers, the retail cost of fresh produce would increase only about 3 percent in the summer-fall season and less than 2 percent in the winter-spring season, because labor represents only a tiny percent of the retail price of produce and because without migrant workers, America would probably import more foreign fruits and vegetables. "The question is whether we want to import more produce from abroad, or more workers from abroad to pick our produce," Huffman remarks.

For American farmers, the answer has been to keep importing workers—which has now made the farmers more vulnerable to foreign competition, since even minimum-wage immigrant workers can't compete with produce picked on farms in China, Chile, or Turkey and shipped here cheaply. A flood of low-priced Turkish raisins several years ago produced a glut in the United States that sharply drove down prices and knocked some farms out of business, shrinking total acreage in California devoted to the crop by one-fifth, or some 50,000 acres. The farms that survived are now moving to mechanize swiftly, realizing that no amount of cheap immigrant labor will make them competitive.

Meager Contribution to Economy

As foreign competition and mechanization shrink manufacturing and farmworker jobs, low-skilled immigrants are likely to wind up farther on the margins of our economy, where many already operate. For example, although only about 12 percent of construction workers are foreign-born, 100,000 to 300,000 illegal immigrants have carved a place for themselves as temporary workers on the fringes of the industry. In urban areas like New York and Los Angeles, these mostly male illegal immigrants gather on street corners, in empty lots, or in Home Depot parking lots to sell their labor by the hour or the day, for $7 to $11 an hour.

That's far below what full-time construction workers earn, and for good reason. Unlike the previous generations of immigrants who built America's railroads or great infrastructure projects like New York's bridges and tunnels, these day laborers mostly do home-improvement projects. A New York study, for instance, found that four in ten employers who hire day laborers are private homeowners or renters wanting help with cleanup chores, moving, or landscaping. Another 56 percent were contractors, mostly small, nonunion shops, some owned by immigrants themselves, doing short-term, mostly residential work. The day laborers' market, in other words, has turned out to be a boon for homeowners and small contractors offering their residential clients a rock-bottom price, but a big chunk of the savings comes because low-wage immigration has produced such a labor surplus that many of these workers are willing to take jobs without benefits and with salaries far below industry norms.

Because so much of our legal and illegal immigrant labor is concentrated in such fringe, low-wage employment, its overall impact on our economy is extremely small. A 1997 National Academy of Sciences [NAS] study estimated that immigration's net benefit to the American economy raises the average income of the native-born by only some $10 billion a year—about $120 per household. And that meager contribution is not the result of immigrants helping to build our essential industries or making us more competitive globally but instead merely delivering our pizzas and cutting our grass. Estimates by pro-immigration forces that foreign workers contribute much more to the economy, boosting annual gross domestic product by hundreds of billions of dollars, generally just tally what immigrants earn here, while ignoring the offsetting effect they have on the wages of native-born workers.

Growing Costs

If the benefits of the current generation of migrants are small, the costs are large and growing because America's vast range of social programs and the wide advocacy network that strives to hook low-earning legal and illegal immigrants into these programs. A 1998 National Academy of Sciences study found that more than 30 percent of California's foreign-born were on [the low-income health program] Medicaid—including 37 percent of all Hispanic households—compared with 14 percent of native-born households. The foreign-born were more than twice as likely as the native-born to be on welfare, and their children were nearly five times as likely to be in means-tested government lunch programs. Native-born households pay for much of this, the study found, because they earn more and pay higher taxes—and are more likely to comply with tax laws. Recent immigrants, by contrast, have much lower levels of income and tax compliance (another study estimated that only 56 percent of illegals in California have taxes deducted from their earnings, for instance). The study's conclusion: immigrant families cost each native-born household in California an additional $1,200 a year in taxes.

Immigration's bottom line has shifted so sharply that in a high-immigration state like California, native-born residents are paying up to ten times more in state and local taxes than immigrants generate in economic benefits. Moreover, the cost is only likely to grow as the foreign-born population—which has already mushroomed from about 9 percent of the U.S. population when the NAS studies were done in the late 1990s to about 12 percent today—keeps growing. And citizens in more and more places will feel the bite, as immigrants move beyond their traditional settling places. From 1990 to 2005, the number of states in which immigrants make up at least 5 percent of the population nearly doubled from 17 to 29, with states like Arkansas, South Dakota, South Carolina, and Georgia seeing the most growth. This sharp turnaround since the

1970s, when immigrants were less likely to be using the social programs of the Great Society than the native-born population, says Harvard economist Borjas, suggests that welfare and other social programs are a magnet drawing certain types of immigrants—nonworking women, children, and the elderly—and keeping them here when they run into difficulty. . . .

Lagging Behind

Almost certainly, immigrants' participation in our social welfare programs will increase over time, because so many are destined to struggle in our workforce. Despite our cherished view of immigrants as rapidly climbing the economic ladder, more and more of the new arrivals and their children face a lifetime of economic disadvantage, because they arrive here with low levels of education and with few work skills—shortcomings not easily overcome. Mexican immigrants, who are up to six times more likely to be high school dropouts than native-born Americans, not only earn substantially less than the native-born median, but the wage gap persists for decades after they've arrived. A study of the 2000 census data, for instance, shows that the cohort of Mexican immigrants between 25 and 34 who entered the United States in the late 1970s were earning 40 to 50 percent less than similarly aged native-born Americans in 1980, but 20 years later they had fallen even further behind their native-born counterparts. Today's Mexican immigrants between 25 and 34 have an even larger wage gap relative to the native-born population. Adjusting for other socioeconomic factors, Harvard's Borjas and Katz estimate that virtually this entire wage gap is attributable to low levels of education.

Meanwhile, because their parents start off so far behind, the American-born children of Mexican immigrants also make slow progress. First-generation adult Americans of Mexican descent studied in the 2000 census, for instance, earned 14 percent less than native-born Americans. By contrast, first-generation Portuguese Americans earned slightly more than the average native-born worker—a reminder of how quickly immigrants once succeeded in America and how some still do. But Mexico increasingly dominates our immigration flows, accounting for 43 percent of the growth of our foreign-born population in the 1990s.

One reason some ethnic groups make up so little ground concerns the transmission of what economists call "ethnic capital," or what we might call the influence of culture. More than previous generations, immigrants today tend to live concentrated in ethnic enclaves, and their children find their role models among their own group. Thus the children of today's Mexican immigrants are likely to live in a neighborhood where about 60 percent of men dropped out of high school and now do low-wage work, and where less than half of the population speak English fluently, which might explain why high school dropout rates among Americans of Mexican ancestry are two and a half times higher than dropout rates for all other native-born Americans, and why first-generation Mexican Americans do not move up the economic ladder nearly as quickly as the children of other immigrant groups. . . .

Setting Limits

If America is ever to make immigration work for our economy again, it must reject policies shaped by advocacy groups trying to turn immigration into the next civil rights cause or by a tiny minority of businesses seeking cheap labor subsidized by the taxpayers. Instead, we must look to other developed nations that have focused on luring workers who have skills that are in demand and who have the best chance of assimilating. Australia, for instance, gives preferences to workers grouped into four skilled categories: managers, professionals, associates of professionals, and skilled laborers. Using a straightforward "points calculator" to determine who gets in, Australia favors immigrants between the ages of 18 and 45 who speak English, have a post-high school degree or training in a trade, and have at least six months' work experience as everything from laboratory technicians to architects and surveyors to information-technology workers. Such an immigration policy goes far beyond America's employment-based immigration categories, like the H1-B visas, which account for about 10 percent of our legal immigration and essentially serve the needs of a few Silicon Valley [computer] industries.

Immigration reform must also tackle our family-preference visa program, which today accounts for two-thirds of all legal immigration and has helped create a 40-year waiting list. Lawmakers should narrow the family-preference visa program down to spouses and minor children of U.S. citizens and should exclude adult siblings and parents.

America benefits even today from many of its immigrants, from the Asian entrepreneurs who have helped revive inner-city Los Angeles business districts to Haitians and Jamaicans who have stabilized neighborhoods in Queens and Brooklyn to Indian programmers who have spurred so much innovation in places like Silicon Valley and Boston's Route 128. But increasingly over the last 25 years, such immigration has become the exception. It needs once again to become the rule.

Immigrants Help the U.S. Economy

Daniel Griswold

Daniel Griswold is director of the Cato Institute's Center for Trade Policy Studies. His October 2002 paper, "Willing Workers: Fixing the Problem of Illegal Mexican Migration to the United States" was used in the Flake-Kolbe-McCain immigration bill in 2003, which President George W. Bush drew upon as the basis for his guest-worker program. In the following article, taken from a 2007 issue of Cato's Free Trade Bulletin, *Griswold proposes that the economic burden of illegal immigration has been exaggerated by opponents of immigration reform. He argues that while low-skilled workers who immigrate to the United States consume more in government services than they pay in taxes, they ultimately help grow the economy by expanding the workforce base and becoming consumers. According to Griswold, it is sensible to foster practical reforms that will enable these immigrants, and their more assimilated children, to better contribute to the U.S. marketplace.*

One frequently heard criticism of comprehensive immigration reform is that it will prove too costly to taxpayers. The mostly low-skilled workers who would be admitted and legalized under the leading reform plan ... considered by the U.S. Congress [in 2007] would typically pay fewer taxes than native-born Americans and presumably consume more means-tested welfare services. Critics of reform argue that legalizing several million undocumented workers and allowing hundreds of thousands of new workers to enter legally each year will ultimately cost American taxpayers billions of dollars.

One recent study from the Heritage Foundation, for example, claims that each "low-skilled household" (one headed by a high-school dropout) costs federal taxpayers $22,000 a year. Spread out over 50 years of expected work, the lifetime cost of such a family balloons to $1.1 million. If immigration reform increases the number of such households in the United States, it will allegedly cost U.S. taxpayers several billion dollars a year.

It is certainly true that low-skilled workers do, on average, consume more in government services than they pay in taxes, especially at the state and local levels. But some of the estimates of that cost have been grossly exaggerated. Moreover, the value of an immigrant to American society should not be judged solely on his or her fiscal impact.

Economic Studies

The wilder estimates of the fiscal impact of low-skilled immigrants are contradicted by more credible estimates. In May 2006 the Congressional Budget Office [CBO] calculated that the 2006 Comprehensive Immigration Reform Act then before the U.S. Senate would have a positive impact of $12 billion on the federal budget during the decade after passage. The 2006 legislation, like [the 2007] proposals, would have allowed low-skilled foreign-born workers to enter the United States through a temporary worker program, and it would have allowed several million undocumented workers in the United States to obtain legal status.

Specifically, the CBO estimated that federal spending would increase $53.6 billion during the period 2007–2016 if the legislation became law, primarily because of increases in refundable tax credits and Medicaid spending. The additional spending would be more than offset in the same period by an even greater increase in federal revenues of $65.7 billion, mostly due to higher collections of income and Social Security taxes but also because of increased visa fees.

One frequently cited figure on the cost of low-skilled immigrants comes from the authoritative 1997 National Research

Council [NRC] study, *The New Americans: Economic, Demographic, and Fiscal Effects of Immigration.* The study calculated the lifetime fiscal impact of immigrants with different educational levels. The study expressed the impact in terms of net present value (NPV), that is, the cumulative impact in future years expressed in today's dollars. The study estimated the lifetime fiscal impact of a typical immigrant without a high school education to be a negative NPV of $89,000. That figure is often cited by skeptics of immigration reform.

A Different Fiscal Picture

What is less often considered is that the NRC study also measured the fiscal impact of the descendants of immigrants. That gives a much more accurate picture of the fiscal impact of low-skilled immigrants. It would be misleading, for example, to count the costs of educating the children of an immigrant without considering the future taxes paid by the educated children once they have grown and entered the workforce. The children of immigrants typically outperform their parents in terms of educational achievement and income. As a result, the NRC calculated that the descendants of a typical [low-skilled] immigrant have a positive $76,000 fiscal impact, reducing the net present value of the fiscal impact of a low-skilled immigrant and descendants to $13,000.

Even that figure does not give the full picture. As the NRC study was being written, Congress passed the 1996 Personal Responsibility and Work Opportunity Reconciliation Act, otherwise know as the 1996 Welfare Reform Act. The act contains an entire title devoted to restricting immigrant access to means-tested welfare, limiting access of noncitizens to such public benefit programs as food stamps and Medicaid. When the NRC study accounted for the impact of the 1996 Welfare Reform Act, the fiscal impact of a single low-skilled immigrant and descendants was further reduced to $5,000 in terms of net present value.

If we accept the NRC estimates, then allowing an additional 400,000 low-skilled immigrants to enter the United States each year would have a one-time NPV impact on federal taxpayers of $2 billion. That cost, while not trivial, would need to be compared to the efficiency gains to the U.S. economy from a larger and more diverse supply of workers and a wider range of more affordable goods and services for native-born Americans. In a post–September 11 security environment, comprehensive immigration reform could also reduce federal spending now dedicated to apprehending illegal economic immigrants.

Roads and Schools

Increased immigration has also been blamed for crowded roads, hospitals, public schools, and prisons. In all four of those cases, the negative impact of immigration has been exaggerated.

As for congestion of roads, immigration has played a secondary role in population growth nationally and at a more local level. Nationally, net international migration accounts for 43 percent of America's annual population growth, with natural growth still accounting for a majority of the growth. On a local level, an analysis of U.S. Census data shows that, for a typical U.S. county, net international migration accounted for 28 percent of population growth between 2000 and 2006. Natural growth from births over deaths accounted for 38 percent of growth on a county level and migration from other counties 34 percent. One-third of U.S. counties actually lost population between 2000 and 2006 as birthrates continue to fall and Americans migrate internally to the most economically dynamic metropolitan areas. If local roads seem more crowded, it is not typically immigration but natural growth and internal migration that are mostly responsible.

As for alleged overcrowding at public schools, [low-skilled] immigrants cannot be singled out for blame. Enrollment in the public school system has actually been declining relative to the size of America's overall population. The share of our population in K–12 public schools has fallen sharply in recent decades, from 22 percent of the U.S. population in 1970 to 16 percent today. As with roads, overcrowding in certain school districts is more likely to be driven by new births and internal migration than by newly arrived immigrants.

Jails and Hospitals

As for crime and the inmate population, again, immigration is not the major driver. Indeed, the violent crime rate in the United States has actually been trending down in recent years as immigration has been increasing. After rising steadily from the 1960s through the early 1990s, the rate of violent crime in the United States dropped from 758 offenses per 100,000 population in 1991 to 469 offenses in 2005. As a recent study by the Immigration Policy Center [IPC] concluded, "Even as the undocumented population has doubled since 1994, the violent crime rate in the United States has declined 34.2 percent and the property crime rate has fallen 26.4 percent."

Immigrants are less likely to be jailed than are their native-born counterparts with similar education and ethnic background. The same IPC study found that "for every ethnic group without exception, incarceration rates among young men are lowest for immigrants, even those who are least educated." Other studies reveal that immigrants are less prone to crime, not because they fear deportation, but because of more complex social factors. All the available evidence contradicts the misplaced fear that allowing additional low-skilled immigrants to enter the United States will somehow increase crime and incarceration rates.

As for hospitals, especially emergency rooms, the presence of uninsured, low-skilled workers in a particular area does impose additional costs on hospitals in the form of uncompensated care. There is no evidence, however, that illegal immigration is the principal cause of such costs nationwide. Indeed, low-skilled immigrants tend to underuse health care because they are typically young and relatively healthy.

A recent report from the Rand Corporation found that immigrants to the United States use relatively few health services. The report estimates that all levels of government in the United States spend $1.1 billion a year on health care for undocumented workers aged 18 to 64. That compares to a total of $88 billion in government funds spent on health care for all adults in the same age group. In other words, while illegal immigrants account for about 5 percent of the workforce, they account for 1.2 percent of spending on public health care for all working-age Americans.

Impact on State and Local Governments

Although the fiscal impact of low-skilled immigrants has been exaggerated by opponents of reform, it can impose real burdens at a local level, particularly where immigration inflows are especially heavy. The 1997 National Research Council study found that, although the fiscal impact of a typical immigrant and his or her descendants is strongly positive at the federal level, it is negative at the state and local level.

State and local fiscal costs, while real, must be weighed against the equally real and positive effect of immigration on the overall economy. Low-skilled immigrants allow important sectors of the U.S. economy, such as retail, cleaning, food preparation, construction, and other services, to expand to meet the needs of their customers. They help the economy produce a wider array of more affordably priced goods and services, raising the real wages of most Americans. By filling gaps in the U.S. labor market, such immigrants create investment opportunities and employment for native-born Americans. Immigrants are also consumers, increasing demand for American-made goods and services.

Several state-level studies have found that the increased economic activity created by lower-skilled, mostly Hispanic immigrants far exceeds the costs to state and local governments. A 2006 study by the Kenan Institute of Private Enterprise at the University of North Carolina at Chapel Hill found that the rapidly growing population of Hispanics in the state, many of them undocumented immigrants, had indeed imposed a net cost on the state government of $61 million, but the study also found that those same residents had increased the state's economy by $9 billion.

A 2006 study by the Texas comptroller of public accounts reached a similar conclusion. Examining the specific fiscal impact of the state's 1.4 million undocumented immigrants, the study found that they imposed a net fiscal cost on Texas state and local governments of $504 million in 2005. The fiscal cost, however, was dwarfed by the estimated positive impact on the state's economy of $17.7 billion.

Policy Solutions

The right policy response to the fiscal concerns about immigration is not to artificially suppress labor migration but to control and reallocate government spending. The 1996 Welfare Reform Act was a step in the right direction. It recognized that welfare spending was undermining the long-term interests of low-income households in the United States, whether native-born or immigrant, by discouraging productive activity. The law led to a dramatic decrease in the use of several major means-tested welfare programs by native-born and immigrant households alike. Further restrictions on access to welfare for temporary and newly legalized foreign-born workers would be appropriate.

Another appropriate policy response would be some form of revenue sharing from the federal to state and local governments. The federal government could compensate state and local governments that are bearing especially heavy up-front costs due to the increase in low-skilled immigration. The transfers could offset additional costs for emergency room health care services and additional public school enrollment. Such a program would not create any new programs or additional government spending; it would simply reallocate government revenues in a way that more closely matched related spending.

Misplaced apprehensions about the fiscal impact of immigration do not negate the compelling arguments for comprehensive immigration reform, nor do they justify calls for more spending on failed efforts to enforce our current dysfunctional immigration law. If the primary goal is to control the size of government spending, then Congress and the president should seek to wall off the welfare state, not our country.

Illegal Immigrants Are Costing Public Schools Too Much

Jack Martin

The following 2005 report comes from the Federation for American Immigration Reform (FAIR), a nonprofit organization advocating tighter immigration controls and a halt to illegal immigration. Jack Martin, who joined FAIR in 1995, is the director of special projects and has testified before the U.S. Congress, U.S. Civil Rights Commission, and U.S. Commission on Immigration Reform. In the report, Martin argues that educating illegal immigrants has become an enormous, and insupportable, expenditure for many states. While students' parents may offset some of these costs by paying taxes, the author notes, illegal immigrants use much more in the way of public services than they support. Martin presents a series of alternative spending scenarios for individual states that are most burdened by these costs in order to demonstrate that these extra expenses have worrisome consequences for native-born students. Finally, Martin makes the case for tighter federal restrictions on illegal immigration in order to reduce this spending.

With states straining under gaping budget shortfalls, public schools throughout the country are facing some of the most significant decreases in state education funding in decades. In some states, drastic cuts mean lay-offs for teachers, larger class sizes, fewer textbooks, and eliminating sports, language programs, and after-school activities. Nearly two-thirds of the states have cut back or proposed reductions in support for childcare and early childhood programs. Some are even shortening the school week from five days to four.

While these massive budget deficits cannot be attributed to any single source, the enormous impact of large-scale ille-

Jack Martin, "Breaking The Piggy Bank: How Illegal Immigration Is Sending Schools Into The Red," www.fairus.org, June 2005. Reproduced by permission.

gal immigration cannot be ignored. *The total K-12 school expenditure for illegal immigrants costs the states nearly $12 billion annually, and when the children born here to illegal aliens are added, the costs more than double to $28.6 billion.*

This enormous expenditure of the taxpayers' hard-earned contributions does not, however, represent the total costs. Special programs for non-English speakers are an additional fiscal burden as well as a hindrance to the overall learning environment. A recent study found that dual language programs represent an additional expense of $290 to $879 per pupil depending on the size of the class. In addition, because these children of illegal aliens come from families that are most often living in poverty, there is also a major expenditure for them on supplemental feeding programs in the schools. Those ancillary expenditures have not been included in the calculations in this report.

The data presented here provide yet one more illustration of the costs of turning a blind eye to illegal immigration and should provide further impetus for states to demand that the federal government finally take effective and decisive action to restore integrity to our nation's immigration laws.

State Costs

The 1.5 million school-aged illegal immigrants residing in the United States and their 2 million U.S.-born siblings can be divided among the states using government estimates of the illegal alien population. Using each state's per-pupil expenditure reported by the U.S. Department of Education, cost estimates for educating illegal immigrants in each state [can be calculated].

The calculation of the number of children of illegal aliens in the K-12 public school system indicates that more than 15 percent of California's students are children of illegal aliens, as are more than ten percent of the students in Arizona, Colorado, Illinois, Nevada, and Texas. More than five percent of the students are the children of illegal aliens in Florida, Georgia, Kansas, New Jersey, New Mexico, New York, North Carolina, Oregon, Rhode Island, Utah, and Washington.

Defenders of illegal aliens assert that the cost of educating illegal alien students is offset by the taxes paid by their parents, but study after study shows that immigrants cost taxpayers much more in public services used than they pay into the system via taxes. This is particularly true of illegal immigrants, who are disproportionately low-skilled and thus low-earning and are much more likely to be working in the underground economy or providing contractual services and not withholding taxes.

Alternative Spending Scenarios

A look at the top ten highest state expenditures provides a stark illustration of the trade-offs for accommodating large-scale illegal immigration:

In California, the $7.7 billion spent annually educating the children of illegal immigrants—nearly 13% of the overall [2004–05] education budget—could:

- Cover the education budget shortfall for the 2004–05 school year, estimated by the Legislative Analyst Office at $6 billion and nearly cover the $2 billion reduction [in 2005] from the Proposition 98 formula.

- Or, the remaining $1.7 billion could pay the salaries of about 31,000 teachers and reduce per student ratios, or it could furnish 2.8 million new computers—enough computers for about half of the state's students.

- Prevent educational shortfalls estimated at $9.8 billion over the past four years that have impacted on "... class size, teacher layoffs, shorter library hours and fewer counselors, nurses, custodians and groundskeepers." (See *Los Angeles Times*, March 11, 2005)

In Texas, the $3.9 billion spent annually educating the children of illegal immigrants could:

- Cover more than the $2.3 billion shortfall identified by the Texas Federation for Teachers for such things as textbooks and pension contributions.

- Make Texas' salaries for teachers more competitive by national standards, thereby reducing costly attrition, and recruit the 5,000 new teachers needed each year.

In New York, the $3.1 billion spent annually educating the children of illegal immigrants could:

- Nearly cover the estimated $3.3 billion required by the state's Supreme Court under the decision in the Campaign for Fiscal Equity case to establish equitable state funding for New York City's public school system.

- Help to reduce the $1.8 billion revenue shortfall for fiscal year 2005 in New York City.

- Provide enough additional funding to nearly meet the $3 billion in health care cuts in the current proposed budget for payments to hospitals and nursing homes.

In Illinois, the $2 billion spent annually educating the children of illegal immigrants could:

- Balance the [2005] state budget—estimated to be $2 billion in the red—and make unnecessary adoption of the new taxes in the Education Funding Reform Act of 2005.

- Help close the potential gap resulting from decreased federal 2006 funding to the state of between $1.07 [and] $1.35 billion.

In New Jersey, the $1.5 billion spent annually educating the children of illegal immigrants could:

- Go a long way toward solving the dilemma Gov. Codey noted on March 1, 2005, when he said, "I wish I could be here discussing a major investment in higher education or an expansion of health care because those are investments New Jersey needs to make, but I can't have those discussions, not with this [fiscal] mess in front of us."

- Help close the potential gap resulting from decreased federal 2006 funding to the state of between $682 [and] $845 million.

In Florida, the $1.2 billion spent annually educating the children of illegal immigrants could:

- Fund the services eliminated as a result of a cut in federal funding to Florida public schools estimated by the Center on Budget and Policy Priorities to be $565 million over the next five years beginning in 2006. Over the same period, the Center estimated an additional $321 million has been lost to the state for adult and vocational education as well as $3.2 billion in grants to the state and local governments and $392 million in "Strengthening America's Communities" block grants.

- Help close the potential gap resulting from decreased federal 2006 funding to the state of between $1.52 [and] $1.89 billion.

In Georgia, the $952 million spent annually educating the children of illegal immigrants could:

- Raise the performance of the state's schools described by Gov. Perdue in his 2003 State of the State Address in these terms, "Georgia's education system is not what it should be. The National Assessment of Education Progress is the nation's education report card. It shows Georgia is behind the national average on reading, writing, math, and science. For each of those subjects more than 50% of Georgia children are below the proficient level. Georgia also has one of the lowest high school graduation rates in the nation. And, to our shame, we rank 50th in SAT scores. We can sum up our report card in two words: 'Needs improvement.'"

- Help close the potential gap resulting from decreased federal 2006 funding to the state of between $847 [and] $1,071 million.

In North Carolina, the $771 million spent annually educating illegal immigrant children could:

- Redress part of a $1.2 billion state budget shortfall and obviate the need for new taxes proposed by Gov. Mike Easley for the 2006 budget.

- Help close the potential gap resulting from decreased federal 2006 funding to the state of between $888 [and] $1,129 million.

In Arizona, the $748 million spent annually educating illegal immigrant children could:

- Improve state funding for education, which in this year's Quality Counts 2005 state-by-state education report ranked Arizona 50th in per-pupil spending. To close the gap with the national average in spending per student would cost the state an additional $1.6 billion.

- Help close the potential gap resulting from decreased federal 2006 funding to the state of between $587 and $763 million.

In Colorado, the $564 million spent annually educating illegal immigrant children could:

- Reduce the state budget deficit estimated at $900 million in the [2003–04] budget, and more recently by the Independence Institute at around $158 million for 2006.

- Help close the potential gap resulting from decreased federal 2006 funding to the state of between $270 and $337 million.

In-State Tuition Discounts

Efforts are underway in several states and in Congress to allow illegal aliens to pay steeply discounted in-state tuition at public colleges and universities—rates not available to American citizens from other states. As state universities across the country increasingly limit enrollment, increasing the intake of illegal aliens into these schools will mean fewer opportunities and less aid for U.S. citizens and legal immigrants. It will also mean a higher cost to the state taxpayers; out-of-state tuition is typically two to 3.5 times higher than in-state tuition.

In 2000, about 126,000 illegal immigrants under 21 were enrolled in college, according to research from the Congressional Research Service. Using 2000 data, we calculated that at non-resident tuition rates, they would be paying between $503 million and $655 million annually. If they were made eligible for in-state tuition discounts, they would be paying less than one-third of that amount, i.e., $155 million to $201 million—leaving taxpayers to make up the difference of $348 million to $454 million.

We estimate that both the number of illegal alien students and the tuition costs will have increased since 2000. In 2004 the estimated outlays would be about $839 million to $1.092 billion, and the discount for in-state tuition would reduce that to about $258 million to $336 million—leaving the taxpayers to make up the difference of $581 million to $756 million. . . .

Proposed federal legislation to give illegal aliens in-state tuition rates would carry additional substantial costs. According to the Congressional Budget Office, making illegal alien students eligible for federal tuition assistance through Pell grants would have cost $195 million in 2003 and $362 million over the 2003–2006 period.

The estimate by the Congressional Budget Office of costs for providing tuition assistance to illegal alien students and the state cost estimates of providing access to in-state tuition at taxpayer expense above do not include the U.S.-born children of illegal aliens because they are already eligible to attend college as in-state residents. However, it should be noted that these expenses, like their education at the primary and secondary level, result from the illegal immigration of their parent(s) and could be avoided if the immigration authorities more effectively deterred illegal immigration and identified and removed those illegally residing in the country.

Reduce Illegal Immigration

All of our children—native-born and immigrants alike—are receiving a poorer education as a result of the federal government passing its immigration law enforcement failures on to the states. The implications for the coming generations of workers, our future economy, and our long-term competitiveness in the world cannot be ignored.

If the federal government remains unwilling to undertake serious enforcement of the United States' immigration laws, it will eventually be forced to provide massive federal education funds to the states. A far more logical and cost-effective alternative—and one with considerable pay-offs in other areas as well—would be to substantially reduce illegal immigration.

Without a serious commitment to doing just that, the open borders and lax enforcement that allow millions of illegal aliens to enter the U.S. ... each year—and to obtain driver's licenses and other official identification documents with virtually no fear of the law—will continue to undermine the will of the American people, overburden our communities' financial resources, and imperil our children's future.

Illegal Immigrants and Their Children Should Be Educated Despite Costs

Houston Chronicle

In this 2006 article from the Houston Chronicle, *described is the impact of the 1982 Supreme Court ruling* Plyler v. Doe, *on the Texas public school system. That decision, which held that schools must educate all students in spite of their immigration status, has had serious financial repercussions on the Texas budget while simultaneously enabling illegal immigrants to seek better futures through higher education. Although the* Houston Chronicle *acknowledges the economic strain of the ruling's legacy, they also interview educators and students who believe that* Plyler *affords hard-working people the opportunity to pursue the American dream.*

After cleaning houses all day, 23-year-old Damaris makes a half-hour trek to the Newcomers Charter School for night classes. She's just a few months away from earning a high school diploma, enrolling in classes at Houston Community College and trying to land a job in the business world.

Working and studying 15 hours a day has not been easy, but Damaris said she knows the effort will give her a chance at a middle-class lifestyle that wouldn't have been possible in Mexico.

"This school changed my life. I have a new opportunity," Damaris, who overstayed her visa a few years, said of the $450,000 program that the Houston Independent School District opened last year at Lee High School to provide night and Saturday classes to about 200 recent immigrants.

Damaris, who asked to be identified by her middle name, and an estimated 1.5 million students in the country illegally—including possibly 20,000 to 35,000 in HISD—can thank a 1982 Supreme Court ruling for opening the doors of public schools to them.

The ruling, which held that young people cannot be denied an education because of immigration status, has changed the face of public school systems in the Houston area and the United States.

Those changes, in turn, have fanned the immigration debate, providing fodder to those who point to the expense of educating such children as a reason to crack down on illegal immigrants. Others maintain that the cost of turning the youngsters away would be far greater.

"If you want to get to the source of animosity, that has to be a part of it," said Edwin S. Rubenstein, an Indiana-based researcher who questions the value of immigration.

Few districts have felt the impact of the historic Supreme Court case, called *Plyler v. Doe*, more than Houston.

In addition to requiring extra books, teachers and classroom space, HISD had to ramp up bilingual instruction, increase social services and develop programs to help countless immigrants catch up academically.

The district created the Newcomers Charter School and even foots the entire bill for some students—such as Damaris—who are too old to qualify for state funding.

Studies put Texas' cost of educating undocumented students as high as $1.65 billion a year, an expense that easily outpaces other costs associated with illegal immigration, such as medical and criminal justice services, experts say.

These students, who often can't speak English when they enroll and are years behind in their studies, are more expensive to educate. Also, their families typically pay less taxes than others—a lopsided equation that critics say adds tension to one of the most controversial issues of the day.

"They're not paying their share of those services merely because they're poorer than most people. They're younger, and they have more children in public school," Rubenstein said. "They are basically subsidized by people who are not immigrants."

Advocates maintain, however, that without a high school education, these students would be less-productive workers and could end up in jail or on welfare.

"Only through education are we going to be able to build a stronger society that will be more productive for the older generation," said Manuel Rodriguez Jr., vice president of the HISD school board. "If we don't educate our kids and we don't have a viable economy, we're not going to have much to look forward to in our golden years."

'Little Schools'

In the mid-1970s, undocumented students attended school in makeshift classrooms at churches and in community centers on the northside and East End of Houston, said Isaias Torres, an attorney who represented undocumented students in the landmark case.

At the "escuelitas"—Spanish for "little schools"—students of all ages crammed into one or two classrooms to study reading, writing and math.

"It was kind of a throwback to the 1930s," Torres said. "The facilities were nothing. (The teachers) were volunteers, but the parents wanted the children to be educated."

At that time, Texas schools either denied admission or required undocumented students to pay out-of-district tuition. Texas schools collected $23 million in tuition in 1982–83— some of which would have been from undocumented students, Texas Education Agency officials said.

A group of undocumented students filed the class-action lawsuit in 1977, seeking the same free public education as U.S.-born children.

The case played out in a district court in Houston, where lawyers representing districts from across the state argued that the influx of undocumented students could ruin public schools.

"So many states, like California, New York and Illinois, they were waiting to see what was going to happen here," Torres said. "There was a lot of interest."

It took about two months to try the case. The ruling to overturn Texas' policy was upheld in appeals to the 5th Circuit in 1980 and then to the Supreme Court in 1982.

Now, because of the protections afforded to immigrants under the ruling, schools don't even try to count how many undocumented students are enrolled.

"There's no reason to ask. Even if you could do it legally, why would you want to?" University of Texas law professor Barbara Hines said. "It has a chilling effect."

Others say that putting numbers and costs on the issue would add depth to the immigration debate.

"We certainly could count. They're just unwilling," said State Board of Education member David Bradley. "We track everything: who eats breakfast and lunch. We track cattle. . . . It'd be kind of nice to see who's going to school and where."

But short of demanding documentation, which many believe would violate the spirit of the Supreme Court ruling, it would be difficult to determine which students are in the country illegally and even which ones are foreign-born.

Many students who primarily speak a language other than English were born in the United States to parents living here illegally. Others entered the country with temporary permits or have won refugee status.

The numbers that are available: 59 percent of HISD's 208,000 students are Hispanic, roughly 60,000 are classified as "Limited English Proficient," and 10,130 students are considered "immigrants"—meaning that they were born outside the U.S. and have been in U.S. schools for three years or less.

The number of Hispanic students in HISD has more than doubled since the 1982 ruling. The district now spends $158 million a year on bilingual and English as a Second Language programs and hires 2,391 teachers—about 20 percent of the teaching staff—for those classes, according to state records.

The cost of illegal immigration to Texas' public schools jumps to about $4 billion a year, according to one study, when the immigrants' children—some of whom were born in the United States and are, therefore, citizens—are counted.

In return, their families contribute nearly $1 billion to the state sales and property tax coffers, according to a study by Jack Martin, special projects director for the Federation for American Immigration Reform, a group that supports tighter restrictions on immigration.

The organization is currently studying the financial impact of immigration on several states.

"It is simply a part of an effort to educate the public to the fact that the advantages that employers are getting from being able to hire low-wage workers are not free. There are very real costs associated with it, and those costs are passed on," Martin said.

In addition to using state and local tax dollars, each student enrolled in a Texas school draws a share of the Permanent School Fund, created more than 150 years ago when Texas was annexed. [In 2005], the state spent $1.6 billion of the $20 billion fund, which is made up of stocks, bonds and the proceeds from land sales, Bradley said.

The money shouldn't be spent educating illegal immigrants, he said.

"These are assets that are owned by the citizens of Texas, and those assets are being distributed and spent on all students," Bradley said.

The influx of immigrants is putting a strain on Texas' public schools, he said.

"It's the immigration isssue, which everybody has kind of not wanted to talk about."

Division of Funds

But watching undocumented students walk out of class this spring—waving Mexican flags and chanting in Spanish—has forced the issue. These students are drawing millions of dollars away from U.S.-born students, critics say.

"I think they diverted resources from other students clearly. I think the gifted-and-talented students are probably at a disadvantage when it comes to fighting for funding," Rubenstein said. "I could see ordinary Anglo-Saxon, American-born people being extremely annoyed that so much of the school district funding is being diverted to serve the immigrant population."

Principal Steve Amstutz, who oversees the 205-student Newcomers program at Lee High, said he hopes the public understands the upside to the *Plyler* ruling.

In many ways, he said, these students are more dedicated and driven than American teens.

"They know how hard it is out there, and they know how much a diploma can help them," Amstutz said. "They know what they want. They have dreams. They want to contribute."

Amstutz said he thinks he can convince critics that these children aren't a drain on his school.

"I always think, and I may be naive, that if you met my kids, you wouldn't feel that way about children," he said. "You want these kids in your business. You want to hire them. They're not asking for anything but a chance."

Damaris, the 23-year-old who's about to graduate, feels the pressure created by the recent immigration debate. Like her undocumented classmates, she watches the news regularly to see how the legislation is progressing.

She wishes there weren't such a backlash against young people who are trying to better their lives.

"I would like to change the mind of the people, but I can't," she said. "The most we can do is to show that we can support ourselves."

Torres said U.S. society has benefited by educating students such as Damaris. The school system hasn't crumbled or been overwhelmed, he said, like educators predicted in a Houston courtroom so many years ago.

"There's been a net profit to the community because they've been in school," Torres said. "It would have been short-sighted to exclude them. They're not going anywhere."

Hispanic Majority

The number of Hispanic students in HISD has more than doubled since a 1982 U.S. Supreme Court ruling required public schools to admit illegal immigrants:

1982–1983

Black: Number of students. . .85,679; Percentage. . .44 percent

Hispanic: Number of students. . .60,193; Percentage. . .31 percent

Anglo: Number of students. . .48,567; Percentage. . .25 percent

Total: Number of students. . .194,439

2004–2005

Black: Number of students. . .60,577; Percentage. . .29 percent

Hispanic: Number of students. . .123,005; Percentage. . .59 percent

Anglo: Number of students. . .18,428; Percentage. . .9 percent

Other: Number of students. . .6,444; Percentage. . .3 percent

Total: Number of students. . .208,454

Source: HISD

Illegal Immigrants Are Abusing the Public Health System

Alison Green and Jack Martin

The following viewpoint proposes that legal and illegal immigrants are straining the U.S. health-care system to the breaking point. The authors, Alison Green and Jack Martin, cite the lack of health insurance among this population for creating spiraling health-care costs for states in the billions of dollars and place an undue burden on American taxpayers. In addition, the authors point to the closure of health facilities and slashed services in states with high immigration as proof that the problem is escalating and having a negative consequence for U.S. citizens requiring medical care. Pushed to make changes, many states are becoming stricter about immigration, say the authors, though not with the vigilance that Green and Martin would like to see. Green and Martin coauthored the viewpoint for the Federation for American Immigration Reform (FAIR), a nonprofit organization advocating tighter immigration controls and a halt to illegal immigration. Green is communications director for Negative Population Growth, a limited-population-growth advocacy organization. Martin is director of special projects for FAIR.

America's health care system is in crisis: The numbers and proportion of the uninsured are rising rapidly. Costs are skyrocketing—2003 saw the largest increase in employer health care costs in 13 years—and posing an increasingly difficult burden on businesses and individuals. At the same time, state budget deficits mean states are cutting back public health care funding, and hospitals around the country are being forced to close or cut back services.

Alison Green and Jack Martin, *The Sinking Lifeboat: Uncontrolled Immigration And The U.S. Health Care System.* Washington, DC: Federation for American Immigration Reform, 2004. Copyright © 2004 FAIR Horizon Press. Reproduced by permission.

In the midst of this crisis, mass immigration is straining the health care system to the breaking point. Indeed, more than half of all counties surveyed by the National Association of Counties say that recent immigration—both legal and illegal—is causing their uncompensated health care costs to rise.

Non-reimbursed costs also get shifted to patients who do have health insurance, thus increasing the cost of care for everyone. High levels of unpaid medical bills also have forced local health care providers to reduce staffing and services and increase rates. Dozens of hospitals in the counties along the southwest border have either closed or face bankruptcy because of losses caused by uncompensated care given to immigrants.

As states cut their health care budgets to try to make ends meet, high rates of immigration are causing a major drain on health care resources and taxpayer funds. Due to lack of enforcement of federal immigration laws, state taxpayers are being forced to fund health care services for illegal aliens at a time when they can't fund all their services for the general population.

But the failures of federal immigration enforcement tell only part of the story. In many areas, the magnitude and cost of illegal immigration are also consequences of state and local policies that encourage illegal alien settlement by granting costly benefits to people who violate immigration laws.

Legislative Initiatives

Under current law, hospitals must treat and stabilize anyone who seeks emergency care, regardless of income, insurance, or immigration status.

Yet most hospitals receive little or no reimbursement for the care to legal and illegal immigrants that the federal government mandates that they provide.

Although the Illegal Immigrant Reform and Immigrant Responsibility Act of 1996 (IIRAIRA) approved reimbursement to hospitals for emergency care for illegal immigrants, as well as reimbursement to state and local governments for ambulance services provided to illegal immigrants injured while crossing the border, neither program has been funded.

In 1997, Congress appropriated $25 million a year for four years to supplement funding for state emergency health services for illegal immigrants, in the twelve states with the highest number of illegal aliens. This program has since terminated. Congress is considering legislation that would create a similar program, but at present no such program is active.

Lawsuits brought by several states against the federal government in the 1990s, seeking reimbursement for the cost of handling the massive influx of illegal aliens that federal authorities had failed to contain, were dismissed on the grounds that the issue was a "political question" and not one for the courts.

The 1996 Personal Responsibility and Work Opportunity Reconciliation Act stopped immigrants from receiving Medicaid for their first five years in the country (with exceptions for those here prior to 1996, children, and pregnant women). However, Congress didn't touch emergency Medicaid, which allows both legal and illegal immigrants to receive emergency medical treatment. (Medicaid funds are drawn from federal, state, and local budgets.)

3.5 million immigrants were enrolled in Medicaid in 2002, and an additional 3.7 million were enrolled in Medicare.

The Uninsured

Our immigration policies have played a significant role in creating our national health care crisis, in which more than 41 million Americans lack basic health insurance.

Immigrants are two and a half times as likely to lack health insurance as natives.

Thirty-three percent of immigrants—one in three—have no insurance (compared to 13 percent of the native-born).

One out of every four uninsured people in the United States is an immigrant, show Census data. (This is a dramatically disproportionate share, as immigrants comprise 11.5 percent of the total population.)

When the National Association of Counties surveyed its members in 2002, 67 percent of counties cited an increase in immigration as a cause of the rise in uncompensated health care expenses and all of the responses indicated that newly arrived immigrants are among the predominant users of uncompensated health care.

Why are immigrants disproportionately uninsured? Because of illegal immigration and because U.S. immigration policy slants toward admitting relatives rather than immigrants with needed workplace skills, our immigration system literally imports poverty. Sixteen percent of all immigrant households live below the poverty level, and one out of every five households of non-citizens is poor (versus eleven percent poverty among native households). The median household income for immigrant households is 13 percent lower than that of native households, and, for the households of non-citizens, it is 23 percent lower.

Among full-time wage earners, 51 percent of non-citizen immigrants had employment-based coverage, compared with 76 percent of naturalized citizens and 81 percent of U.S.-born residents. Among the lowest-wage full-time workers (earning less than $15,000 annually), 27 percent of non-citizen immigrants have employment-based coverage, compared to 58 percent of U.S.-born residents.

The Public Pays

Because of the uncompensated expense of treating uninsured patients, communities with high rates of uninsured residents "are more likely to reduce hospital services, divert public resources away from disease prevention and surveillance programs, and reallocate tax dollars so that they can pay for uncompensated medical care," according to an Institute of Medicine of the National Academies of Sciences report.

In 2001, public funds made up for up to 85 percent of the $34–$38 billion shortfall in unreimbursed expenses incurred by the uninsured.

The problem is on the rise: Immigrants (legal and illegal) who arrived between 1994 and 1998 and their children accounted for 59 percent (2.7 million people) of the growth in the size of the uninsured population since 1993. . . .

Trouble for Taxpayers

Yet it's not only recent immigration contributing to the problem: More than a third (37 percent) of immigrants who entered in the 1980s have still not acquired health insurance, and more than a quarter (27 percent) of immigrants who entered in the 1970s remain uninsured.

When the 3.5 million immigrants receiving insurance through publicly-funded Medicaid are factored in, *almost half of immigrants have either no insurance or have it provided to them at taxpayers' expense.*

Lack of insurance leads many immigrants to forego or postpone medical care, especially preventive care. Because this can cause medical conditions to deteriorate, it often ultimately increases the cost of treatment. Many immigrants end up using hospital emergency departments—the most expensive source of health care—as their primary care provider.

Because emergency rooms must treat patients regardless of their ability to pay, high rates of uninsured patients can spell financial disaster for hospitals. The cost of caring for these patients is absorbed by the counties or hospitals obligated to provide treatment, and some is passed on to insured patients.

Burden on Hospitals

The problem is particularly pronounced in communities near the southwest border, where there are high populations of illegal aliens. Border hospitals reported losses of almost $190 million in unreimbursed costs for treating illegal aliens in 2000 (about one-fourth of the hospitals' total unreimbursed expenses). Had the report included physician and ambulance fees and follow-up services, the total price tag for illegal aliens would have been about $300 million, according to the report's authors.

The U.S.-Mexico Border Counties Coalition studied the 24 counties next to the Mexican border and concluded: "The disproportionate burden placed on southwest border counties for providing emergency healthcare services to (illegal aliens) is compounding an already alarming state of affairs."

In some hospitals, as much as two-thirds of total operating costs are for uncompensated care for illegal aliens. The increase in such costs has forced some hospitals to reduce staff, increase rates, and cut back services.

The problem has become so out of hand that some Mexican ambulance companies are now instructing their drivers to take uninsured patients across the border to the United States. The ambulances simply drive across the U.S.-Mexico border's many unguarded crossings. The National Advisory Committee on Rural Health notes that the drivers face little resistance at border crossings.

States Suffer

Dozens of hospitals in the counties along the border face severe losses caused by uncompensated care provided to uninsured immigrants.

Arizona, facing a $1 billion state budget shortfall in FY [fiscal year] 2004, is considering cutting 60,000 children from of the State Children's Health Insurance Program. Yet in December 2001, the legislature approved $3 million to cover kidney dialysis and chemotherapy for illegal aliens.

- The health department in Cochise County, where the population of illegal aliens is estimated to have increased by 48 percent since 1999, spends almost a third of its budget on care for illegal aliens. At least one hospital there—Southeast Arizona Medical Center—has filed for bankruptcy and is in danger of closing due to uncompensated care for illegal aliens.

- Cochise's Copper Queen Community Hospital spends two-thirds of its operating income on uncompensated care for immigrants, a factor administrators say played a role in the hospital's decision to close its long-term care unit. The facility also has closed its maternity ward because of uncompensated costs. The hospital's emergency room has seen a 20 percent increase in patient volume in the past several years, and the average wait for service has climbed to four to six hours.

- Phoenix's Good Samaritan Regional Medical Center lost $1 million treating illegal immigrants during the first quarter of fiscal year 2002. The wait for intensive care beds there can last several days, and some ER patients have waited 24 hours to see a doctor.

- University Medical Center in Tucson lost $6.5 million in 2000 caring for immigrants, an increase over the previous year's $3.5 million cost. The hospital ended 2000 with a budget shortfall and predicted it would have to absorb $8 to $10 million worth of uncompensated care to foreign nationals in 2002.

- The five largest health care providers in Maricopa County lost $318 million in uncompensated care in 2001. Maricopa Medical has had to delay improvements and double up rooms, putting four patients into rooms built for two.

California, in addition to Emergency Medicaid, provides both legal and illegal aliens with prenatal care, and nursing home care. Additionally, locally funded initiatives in Los Angeles, San Bernardino, San Francisco, San Mateo, and River-side counties now pay for health insurance for illegal immigrants in those jurisdictions.

- In the last decade, 60 California emergency rooms have closed, 19 of them in just the last three years [2001–2004]. In 2000, 289 emergency rooms in California reported operating at a loss. California hospital losses totaled $390 million in 2001, up from $325 million in 2000 and $316 million in 1999. The crisis reaches throughout the state, with 80 percent of emergency departments reporting losses.

- In Santa Cruz, hospitals are so crowded that they regularly close their doors to new emergency patients. When they're open, less urgent patients often have to wait up to ten hours on weekends.

- Scripps Memorial Hospital in Chula Vista estimates that about one quarter of patients who are uninsured and don't pay their bills are illegal aliens. The hospital loses $7 million to $10 million in uncompensated costs.

- Regional Medical Center and Pioneers Memorial Hospital in El Centro, California lost over $1.5 million treating illegal immigrants in 2001.

- 30 to 40 percent of the Community Clinic of Orange County's patients in Santa Ana are illegal immigrants.

Texas, facing a $10 billion two-year state budget shortfall, plans to roll back Medicaid and coverage for children under the State Children's Health Insurance Program to the minimum levels mandated by law. In 2001, Texas attorney general John Cornyn issued a legal opinion stipulating that federal law bans hospitals from using tax dollars to provide non-emergency care to illegal immigrants. However, Harris County—the state's largest county, which includes Houston—

announced it would ignore the opinion and continue to provide taxpayer-subsidized non-emergency care to illegal aliens.

- According to the Texas Hospital Association, Texas hospitals spent $393 million treating illegal aliens in 2002.

- Illegal aliens account for almost one quarter of all visits to facilities in the Harris County Hospital District. The district estimates that it spent $330 million on health care for illegal residents between 1998 and 2000, of which $105 million was reimbursed with federal funds, leaving the remaining $225 million to be paid by taxpayers.

- In El Paso, where nearly 40 percent of residents have no health insurance and the illegal alien problem is rampant, Thomason General Hospital is seeking a 12.5 percent property tax increase to help offset its uncompensated care costs. The facility lost $32 million in uncompensated costs in 2001, not including an additional $49.7 million in charity care for patients whom the hospital knew up front could not pay their bills.

- An administrator at Texas's Brownsville Medical Center estimated that his hospital spends $500,000 a month treating illegal aliens.

In *Florida*, if Medicaid costs continue to increase at the current rate, the costs would consume the entire state budget by 2015.

- According to the Florida Hospital Association, non-citizens amass unpaid bills of more than $40 million a year at Florida hospitals.

- The number of *uninsured* non-U.S. citizens admitted to Florida hospitals nearly doubled between 1997 and 2001, reaching 7,670 in 2001.

- Broward County collects $190 million annually in property taxes to offset the $453 million lost in uncompensated care.

- The Florida Hospital Association reports that hospitals in the state "expended considerable time and effort transferring the patient back to their own country or finding appropriate long-term care. Hospitals frequently paid to return the patient to his/her home country and/or absorbed the cost of any follow up care."

Other Regions

The problem isn't confined to states traditionally thought of as high-immigration-impact areas. For example:

- At Iowa's Buena Vista county hospital, which must now pay for translators on staff, uncompensated health care for immigrants constitutes 25 percent of the total services.

- Hospitals throughout South Carolina say they have been left with at least $4 million in unpaid bills after delivering babies for illegal immigrants who disappear before filing Medicaid paperwork.

- In 2002, Pennsylvania and New Jersey hospitals gave almost $2 billion in free emergency and short-term care to uninsured patients, a large share of whom officials believe are illegal aliens.

- In 2001, Chicago's Children's Memorial Hospital spent more than $650,000 on transplants and post-care treatment without reimbursement for three illegal alien children. Chicago's Alivio Medical Center provides $1 million a year in uncompensated care and estimates that more than half of its 20,000 annual patients are illegal aliens.

- Minnesota county commissioners say that the cost of medical care for uninsured immigrants is too high for local government to bear without federal help and have called on the federal government to shift the financial burden away from local hospitals. Minnesota expects a $4.2 billion budget shortfall over the next two years.

- North Carolina has about $1.4 billion in unreimbursed hospital expenses annually. Each month, a Medicaid emergency services program sees 220 new cases involving immigrants, many of whom are illegal, at a cost of $32 million.

- For each of the last three years [2001–2004], 60 percent of hospitals in New York lost money. State hospitals lost a total of $1.7 billion in uncompensated care. Yet the state is offering free insurance coverage to 167,000 legal immigrants, at a cost of about $10 million.

Travel Costs

Hospitals frequently absorb not only the cost of any follow-up care for illegal alien patients but also pay to return them to the home country. For example, one Florida hospital spent $347,000 to treat one illegal alien patient for respiratory distress, to care for him after he stabilized while a doctor in his home country could be found to accept responsibility for him, and to return him and his wife to Colombia. In another case, the facility spent $150,000 to give an illegal alien surgery for progressive curvature of the spine and then return him and his family to their homeland. The president and chief executive of Jamaica Hospital, in Queens, New York, says the facility sees immigrants head straight to the hospital after arriving in the United States. The hospital has started buying plane tickets and sending some of the ill immigrants back home, sometimes buying extra tickets for nurses to serve as escorts.

Making Cuts

Tennessee has removed 208,000 people from its expanded Medicaid program, including 55,000 children. Connecticut has eliminated Medicaid benefits for 23,000 adults and 7,000 children. Oklahoma has discontinued its "medically needy" program, eliminating Medicaid coverage for 8,300 people who had catastrophic medical costs.

In all, 49 states have implemented Medicaid restrictions for the 2003 fiscal year: 25 states have reduced benefits, including restricting or eliminating dental coverage and inpatient hospital days; 27 states have frozen or reduced provider rates; 45 states have enacted prescription drug cost controls; 27 states have enacted eligibility cuts and restrictions; and 17 states have increased beneficiary co-pays.

Struggling hospitals are curtailing services left and right, closing maternity wards and trauma centers, laying off staff, and limiting the drugs that will be offered to patients. In July 2002, the University of California Medical Center at Irvine announced that it would refuse care to anyone who lives more than a few miles from its facilities (except in emergency cases). In West Virginia, two hospitals have closed their maternity wards and several hospitals no longer have either neurosurgeons to treat head injuries or orthopedists to mend broken bones. In El Paso, some clinics for low-income populations now manage conditions on an outpatient basis that would get an insured patient hospitalized.

Making Changes

Some states are beginning to tackle the problem. In March 2003, Colorado became the first state to remove legal immigrants from Medicaid rolls, saving $2.7 million. Massachusetts is considering following suit by changing Medicaid rules to make 9,500 illegal aliens ineligible, by which it hopes to save $13 million a year. Minnesota is considering health care cuts that would remove 4,500 illegal aliens from the General Assistance Medical Care coverage. New Mexico is considering eliminating some emergency medical services for illegal aliens, to save $2 million.

Washington state, facing a $2.6 billion budget deficit, stopped covering 29,000 illegal aliens with Medicaid in October 2002 and expects to save $25 million a year as a result. However, local hospitals are now footing the bill: Children's Hospital & Regional Medical Center in Seattle paid $200,000 in the following two months to care for 600 illegal alien children. And the state, like eleven others, continues to pay for prenatal care for illegal aliens, at a cost to Washington taxpayers of $23 million a year; state lawmakers also set aside about $20 million in 2002 to provide low-income immigrant families with subsidized health insurance.

Immigrants Are Not Causing the Public Health System to Fail

Meredith L. King

Meredith L. King is a health-policy research analyst at the Center for American Progress, a progressive think tank that champions effective governing to promote the common good. King, who writes frequently on health-care access in the United States, is an advocate of universal health care. In this 2007 article, she looks at five "myths" that she believes misinform the American public about immigrants' role in the U.S. health-care system. From exaggerating the burden of uninsured illegal immigrants on medical costs and services to believing that stricter immigration policies would promote better health for U.S. citizens, misconceptions from politicians and pundits have done a disservice to immigrants and the American public, King contends. According to her, illegal and legal immigrants face many obstacles before receiving medical care in the United States, and are not to blame for skyrocketing health-care costs. On the contrary, King concludes that any effort to reform the U.S. health-care system should reduce barriers to insurance coverage for immigrants, which would also promote improved public safety for all, she maintains.

R estrictionist politicians and talking heads concur that immigrants in the United States are a burden on our health care system. A decade ago this belief contributed to legislation that limited immigrants' access to the health care system. Today, similar sentiments misinform the current debate over immigration reform.

These myths about documented and undocumented immigrants' use of U.S. health care services need to be examined in detail if our nation is going to have a true understanding about the immigrants in the U.S. health care system. The five most prevalent of these myths are:

1. U.S. public health insurance programs are overburdened with documented and undocumented immigrants.
2. Immigrants consume large quantities of limited health care resources.
3. Immigrants come to the United States to gain access to health care services.
4. Restricting immigrants' access to the health care system will not affect American citizens.
5. Undocumented immigrants are "free-riders" in the American health care system.

Impact of Myths

These misconceptions feed a perception that one of the biggest reasons for our nation's failing health care system is the growth of immigration—and not the lack of insurance and skyrocketing health care costs. As a consequence, these myths have influenced policymaking and sparked federal efforts to preclude immigrants' access to the health care system.

Such an effort culminated in the 1996 passage of the Personal Responsibility and Work Opportunity Reconciliation Act, which put a five-year ban on eligibility for Medicaid and other public benefits programs for recent immigrants. These same eligibility restrictions were also included in the State Children's Health Insurance Program [SCHIP], which was enacted in 1997.

Then as part of the Deficit Reduction Act of 2005, the law now [as of 2007] requires U.S. citizens to provide proof of citizenship when applying for Medicaid benefits, with the intention of preventing immigrants from obtaining Medicaid coverage.

As this paper will demonstrate, these myths perpetuate the marginal status of immigrants—for this paper, non-citizens—in the U.S. health care system and promote poor policymaking at all levels of government. These myths need to be subjected to the bright light of objective analysis to better inform critical policy-making decisions on health care reform and immigration reform moving forward.

Myth #1

Myth #1: U.S. public health insurance programs are overburdened with documented and undocumented immigrants.

The misinformation supporting the myth that U.S. public health insurance programs are overburdened with documented and undocumented immigrants has percolated into the American psyche for well over a decade. Yet this belief is not substantiated by the facts.

While low-income citizens depend on Medicaid and SCHIP for health coverage, undocumented immigrants and non-permanent documented immigrants, such as individuals with student or temporary work visas, are not eligible for Medicaid, except limited Medicaid coverage for emergency services. Permanent documented immigrants are eligible for public coverage but are subject to restrictions and stipulations. The Personal Responsibility and Work Opportunity Reconciliation Act of 1996 restricted documented immigrants arriving after August 22, 1996 from federally-matched Medicaid coverage for the first five years in residence.

Prior to this act, permanent documented immigrants had the same access to public benefits such as Medicaid, as did U.S. citizens. Five years after passage of the law, non-elderly immigrant adults had experienced a 36 percent decline in coverage. Today [June 2007], about 40 percent of all documented permanent residents in the United States entered after August 22, 1996 and have been subject to this prohibition.

Children Left Out

This same law had a similar effect on immigrant children. Documented and undocumented immigrant children are more likely to be uninsured than citizen children. Roughly 1.5 million of the 6 million uninsured children who are otherwise eligible for Medicaid or SCHIP are excluded from the programs due to their immigration status.

From 1995 to 2005, the uninsured rate for citizen children declined to 15 percent from 19 percent as Medicaid and SCHIP enrollment increased by 17 percent. In contrast, during this same time period the uninsured rate for documented immigrant children increased to 48 percent from 44 percent, while Medicaid and SCHIP coverage declined by 17 percent.

States' Actions

Recognizing the importance of providing health coverage to the immigrant population, 21 states and the District of Columbia now use state-only funds to offer basic health services to documented children and pregnant women who otherwise would be prohibited from enrolling in a public health insurance program due to the five-year limit. States that traditionally have large populations of immigrants, such as California, New York, and Texas, are among them.

Yet over the past 15 years immigrants are increasingly locating in "new growth" states, such as Arkansas, North Carolina, and Iowa. Most of these states do not offer state-funded coverage to documented immigrant children and pregnant women during their first five years and are therefore leaving these populations vulnerable to health risks.

Restrictions Cause Confusion

Even with the five-year ban on public benefits eligibility for recent documented immigrants, belief that ineligible documented and undocumented immigrants are enrolling in Medicaid and SCHIP continues. On July 1, 2006 as part of the

Deficit Reduction Act of 2005, a federal law was enacted requiring U.S. citizens to present proof of their citizenship and identity, such as a U.S. passport or birth certificate, when they apply for Medicaid coverage or seek to renew their coverage.

While the intent of this law was to keep ineligible immigrants from enrolling in Medicaid, it has increased the administrative burden for U.S. citizens as well as documented immigrants eligible for coverage. Some eligible immigrants believe that they must show proof of citizenship, not just legal status, in order to obtain coverage once otherwise eligible.

As a consequence of these restrictions and stipulations, public sector health expenditures are much less for immigrants enrolled in public health programs such as Medicaid or SCHIP. Twenty-one percent of total medical costs were paid through public sources for native-born citizens, compared to 16 percent for documented and undocumented immigrants. In terms of taxes paid per household, this equates to $56 for health care for documented immigrants and $11 for health care (emergency Medicaid services) for the undocumented.

Myth #2

Myth #2: Immigrants consume large quantities of limited health care resources.

Immigrants are more likely to be uninsured and therefore less likely to consume health care services. Nearly 44 percent of documented immigrants were uninsured in 2005, more than three times the uninsured rate for the native born. There is no accurate data on the number of undocumented immigrants who are uninsured, but chances are very high that the percentage is well beyond 44 percent.

One survey of uninsured California farm workers found that only half of the males and one-third of the females had seen a physician in the past two years, even though nearly one in five had an occupational illness or a chronic health problem such as high blood pressure, high cholesterol serum, or obesity. Chronic diseases account for about 75 percent of health care costs in the United States, which demonstrates that if these individuals had health insurance, they would be better able to manage their health and reduce health care costs for everyone.

Documented immigrant children also face a stark reality. For example, uninsured immigrant children are more likely than their citizen counterparts to lack a usual source of care (51 percent compared to 30 percent) or to go more than one year without seeing a health professional (48 percent compared to 38 percent). Additionally, 52 percent of insured immigrant children had a well-child visit in the past year compared to only 30 percent of uninsured immigrant children. No wonder medical expenditures for immigrant children were 74 percent lower per capita than those for U.S.-born children.

Fewer Services Used

Contrary to popular belief, immigrants also rarely use emergency room services. Cases in point: the metropolitan areas of Miami-Dade [Florida], Phoenix [Arizona], and Orange County, Calif.—all urban areas with large immigrant populations—have much lower rates of emergency room use than do areas with smaller immigrant populations, such as Cleveland [Ohio] and Little Rock [Arkansas].

Additionally, fewer than 10 percent of Mexican immigrants, both documented and undocumented, who had been in the United States for fewer than 10 years reported using an emergency room, compared to 20 percent of native-born whites and Mexican Americans. Immigrants' low use of emergency room services reflects a low use of health care services in general—and more specifically reflects fear among immigrants about using the health care system at all.

Lack of insurance means that individuals are more likely to wait for their health problems to worsen before seeking care. And the statistics on immigrant children illustrate this point. While immigrant children visit the emergency room less often than U.S.-born children, because they are often sicker when seeking care their emergency room expenditures are more than three times higher, suggesting that access to primary and preventive care could have prevented the illness from worsening and ultimately, reduced medical costs.

In addition to limited access to emergency room care, immigrants have access to health care services through federally funded community health centers, migrant health centers, promotora programs (Hispanic lay health worker programs), federal grant programs for community initiatives, and other local and state efforts. In 2004, for example, migrant health centers served over 675,000 migrant and seasonal farmworkers. While these programs are effective in delivering health care services to some immigrants their limited capacity and their dependence on limited federal grants and funds for operation do not meet the needs of a growing, diverse immigrant population.

Myth #3

Myth #3: Immigrants come to the United States to gain access to health care services.

Job opportunities across the country are the "magnet" that draws immigrants to the country; not federal incentives such as health care coverage and services. Immigrants are most likely to be employed in industries that do not offer health insurance coverage, such as agriculture, construction, food processing, restaurants, and hotel services. Immigrants are nearly four times more likely to work in the agricultural industry and two times more likely to work in the construction industry. Uninsured rates in these industries are over 30 percent for all workers compared to 19 percent for workers across all industries.

Guest-Worker Programs

Work opportunities through guest-worker programs also drive immigration. Yet the guest-worker programs for temporary, unskilled labor (the H-2A program for agriculture workers and the H-2B program for non-agriculture workers) provide limited, if any, health care benefits to the documented immigrants in the programs.

Immigrants in the H-2A program do have limited legal protections, including employer compensation benefits for medical costs and payment for lost time due to temporary or permanent work injury. But agricultural employers in this program are not required to provide health insurance or other needed services. And existing protections are rarely enforced.

Immigrants in the H-2B programs do not even have those limited benefits. Their employers are obligated to offer full-time work and pay the prevailing wage rate, but there is no regulation requiring any of the benefits afforded H-2A workers.

And while it may seem that H-2A workers have limited access to the health care system on paper, in practice they often find that they do not. These laborers often toil in two of the most dangerous industries, agriculture and forestry. Fatality rates in these two industries are nearly 10 times the national average. Yet both H-2A and H-2B workers often do not have health insurance to cover appropriate care. Even worse, if an injury or illness is severe, immigrant workers in these two programs lose their jobs and therefore their legal status to stay in the United States.

Day Workers

Immigrant day workers experience a similar fate. A 2003–2004 national survey of predominantly undocumented day workers found a high level of occupational injuries. One-fifth of the day laborers had suffered a work-related injury, but less than half received medical care for their injuries.

Purchasing health insurance through the private market is an unlikely option for immigrants as well. The unskilled work of many immigrants is often low-wage; day workers were unlikely to have annual earnings that exceeded $15,000 and full-time immigrant workers averaged $23,000 in annual income in 2003. Yet the average annual premiums cost paid by a worker for individual employer coverage was $508 and for family coverage was $2412 that same year.

Myth #4

Myth #4: Restricting immigrants' access to the health care system will not affect American citizens.

Restricting undocumented and documented immigrants' access to the U.S. health care system threatens our nation's public health. When immigrants arrive in the U.S. they are more likely to be healthier than native born individuals, yet as time goes on, their health deteriorates.

Poorer Public Health

In New York City, for example, immigrants had similar or lower death rates from the 10 leading causes of death in the city compared to U.S. born adults. Four or more years later, however, immigrants to New York City have poorer health than more recent arrivals (24 percent versus 17 percent) and they are more likely to be obese (16 percent versus 12 percent).

Some of this difference can be explained by a change in health behaviors, but an equally important factor is the lack of health insurance. Specifically, the lack of coverage for preventive health services during their initial years in the U.S. is very costly to the nation's overall public health. Additionally, providing preventive services will reduce health care costs in the long run.

Areas with relatively high uninsured rates are likely to have greater instances of vaccine-preventable diseases, communicable diseases, and disability. For example, under-immunization increases a community's vulnerability to outbreaks of diseases such as measles, flu, and pneumonia. Furthermore, childhood and adult immunization levels are positively correlated with having either public or private health insurance.

Cost-Shifting

Even though immigrants use health care services less and therefore have low health care expenditures, the cost of the limited resources uninsured immigrants do use are shifted onto federal and state governments, local communities, and American citizens.

Uncompensated health care received by documented and undocumented immigrants in hospitals is reimbursed by the federal government. State and local governments or charitable entities that are disproportionately affected by uninsurance, such as those delivering health care services in areas with a high density of lower-wage and service-sector jobs, often have a smaller tax base with which to address the health care needs of uninsured residents.

Individuals with insurance, citizens or immigrants, also experiences this cost-shift. In 2005, health insurance premiums for a family of four were $922 higher and individual health insurance premiums were $341 higher due to the cost of health care for the uninsured. Cost-shifting is a consequence of the entire uninsured population, not just the uninsured immigrant population.

Myth #5

Myth #5: Undocumented immigrants are "free riders" in the American health care system.

This myth is perhaps the most ardently asserted belief regarding undocumented immigrants and the U.S. health care system. The facts illustrate that undocumented workers contribute more to the revenue stream for U.S. social benefits than they use.

No "Free Ride"

In Texas, for example, nearly seven percent of the state's population was comprised of undocumented immigrants in 2005. The state's health care costs for undocumented immigrants that same year were a mere $58 million. Yet state revenues collected from undocumented immigrants exceeded what the state spent on social services provided to these immigrants such as health care and education by $424.7 million.

Immigrant contributions to social services are similar across the country. The National Research Council concluded that immigrants will pay on average $80,000 per capita more in taxes than they will use in government services over their lifetimes.

Additionally, in March 2005, more than seven million undocumented immigrants were in the workforce yet received few public services for their labor and tax contributions. The Social Security Administration [SSA], for example, reaps an enormous benefit from the taxes paid by undocumented immigrants. It estimates that workers without valid social security numbers contribute $7 billion in Social Security tax revenues and roughly $1.5 billion in Medicare taxes annually, yet elderly immigrants rarely qualify for Medicare or long-term care services provided through Medicaid.

In 2001, the Social Security Administration concluded that undocumented immigrants "account for a major portion of the billions of dollars paid into social security that don't match SSA records," which payees, many of whom are undocumented immigrants, can never draw upon. As of July 2003, these payments totaled $421 billion.

System Hostile to Immigrants

A close examination of immigrants' actual experience with the U.S. health care system sheds light on the many obstacles immigrants encounter when they seek health insurance and health care. Low-income documented immigrants must wait five years before being eligible for public health insurance. And less than half of the states provide coverage to select documented immigrant populations, such as children and pregnant women.

Furthermore, cumbersome administrative regulations regarding proof of citizenship status dissuade potentially eligible documented immigrants from applying to Medicaid and SCHIP. And although undocumented immigrants contribute to the economy through their labor and taxes, they are barred from federally-matched Medicaid services.

But that is not all. Documented and undocumented immigrants are almost always unable to access employer-based or private health insurance. The reason: the average health insurance premium for a family of four was roughly $11,500, nearly half of the average annual income of an immigrant worker.

Because of these limitations and restrictions, documented and undocumented immigrants are more likely to go without needed medical services and preventive health care, jeopardize health and welfare, and create some cost-shifting.

The increase of documented and undocumented immigrants into the U.S. is not the cause of the failing health care system. The health care system is broken in large part because 45 million individuals lack health insurance and health care premiums have nearly doubled over the past six years. [Any effort to reform the American health-care system should work to reduce barriers to health insurance coverage for immigrants. And any effort at immigration reform should also be informed by these facts.]

CHAPTER 3

Political Responses to Illegal Immigration

Immigration Legislation Should Not Reward Illegal Immigrants

Rep. Mike Pence

Mike Pence is a member of the United States House of Representatives, representing Indiana's Sixth District since 2000. In the following article, Pence makes the case for the Border Integrity and Immigration Reform Act, arguing that many of the other proposals offered by President George W. Bush and members of Congress offer little more than amnesty for illegal immigrants. Pence acknowledges that the United States has always been a country of immigrants and a welcoming nation. However, he maintains, the United States also has a foundation of law and order. Pence argues that the government's role in immigration reform should be limited to border security and law enforcement. He believes that U.S. business, not the government, could more efficiently handle a temporary-worker program. His argument is that illegal immigrants would be happy to self-deport if they knew that U.S. jobs were available to them through work visas awarded by private industry. The Border Integration Reform Act was never brought to the floor of the House of Representatives for a vote.

I agree with the President [George W. Bush] that a rational middle ground can be found between amnesty and mass deportation, but I disagree with the President that amnesty is the middle ground. In the coming days I will introduce the Border Integrity and Immigration Reform Act, which, ... sets forth a *real* rational middle ground between amnesty and mass deportations.

Rep. Mike Pence, "Border Security and Immigration: Building a Principled Consensus for Reform," *Heritage Lectures*, May 23, 2006. Reproduced by permission of the author.

The Border Integrity and Immigration Reform Act is a bill that is tough on border security and tough on employers who hire illegal aliens, but recognizes the need for a guest worker program that operates without amnesty and without growing into a huge new government bureaucracy. I believe that it is a strong alternative to the various amnesty plans being debated by the Senate and pushed by the President, and I hope that it will serve as an attractive alternative for many Members of the House. . . .

Illegal Immigration Threatens the United States

Every night Americans see news images of people crossing the border illegally; they hear tales of people paying thousands of dollars to so-called coyotes to smuggle them into the country; they worry that drugs will make their way into the hands of their children more readily; and they rightly fear that our porous borders make it more likely that terrorists with deadly intentions will cross to inflict harm on our families and communities.

In 2005, Customs and Border Protection officers stopped 1,189,114 people from illegally crossing the border. Of that number, approximately 165,000 were from countries other than Mexico. Over 200 were from Middle Eastern countries such as Afghanistan, Iran, Iraq, Pakistan, and Saudi Arabia, to name just a few.

The Pew Hispanic Center estimates that 12 million illegal aliens are currently living in America. Just a few months [earlier], that estimate was 11 million. In a few more months or years, that estimate could grow to 13, 14, 15, 20 or more million illegal aliens, unless we take action to turn the tide.

We must do something, because this is a problem of epic proportions. It is a problem that threatens the very fabric of America. Every time I am home in Indiana, I hear about this issue from my constituents. Hoosiers are concerned. Americans are concerned. I am concerned.

First and foremost, let us be clear on this point: We can control our borders. At the same time, we can find a *real* rational middle ground for dealing with the illegal immigrants currently in America. A lot of people in Washington are talking about what we can do, but the solutions they are offering, up to this point, are not workable and they are not acceptable to millions of hard-working Americans who believe in law and order and the American Dream.

The Senate is debating a bill that will provide amnesty to millions of illegal aliens. Amnesty is no solution. It only will worsen the problem because it will cause more people to come here illegally with the hope of someday having their status adjusted.

A Nation of Borders

On border security, the House of Representatives got off to a great start in December 2005 when we passed H.R. 4437, the Border Protection, Antiterrorism and Illegal Immigration Control Act of 2005. The Judiciary Committee and the Homeland Security Committee were able to put together a strong bill that will secure our borders.

The House-passed bill was a first step. In fact, my bill begins by including the House bill, with a couple of minor changes. The House got it right, and aside from removing the felony provision for illegal presence and clarifying that no one is trying to put Good Samaritans behind bars, I am keeping this language as is. We must take a tough approach on securing this nation's borders. I have said it once today and will say it again: A nation without borders is not a nation.

Therefore, we must make America a nation with borders. We must man the door. I believed that in December 2005 when I voted for the House bill, and I believe it now.

The President called for 6,000 more Border Patrol agents and the use of the National Guard in the interim. I welcome that call and support it, but it is not enough. The House-passed bill adds port of entry inspectors, ends catch and release, puts to use American technology such as unmanned aerial vehicles, and requires the building of a security fence across approximately 700 miles of our south-western border.

These are the kind of actions that will bring about a new day on our border. Instead of "coyotes," drug-runners, and criminals ruling the border, American law enforcement will rule the border. Instead of terrorists having the ability to sneak through a porous border, they will find a secure border hardened to prevent their illegal entry.

Securing Our Borders

However, as I have been thinking about securing our border, a thought kept coming back to me. So many of the people crossing the border are not crossing for nefarious or devious reasons. The great majority of illegal border crossers do so in order to find work or to be with family members working in America.

I have come to believe that securing the border would be much easier and allow for a better use of our resources if we could eliminate these people from the ranks of those crossing the border illegally. The House bill will secure our border, but it will do it even better when its provisions can concentrate just on those illegal border crossers who are criminals, drug dealers, and possible terrorists. In order to do that, there must be a legal means for the great majority of people seeking to come to America to work temporarily.

A few months ago a very dedicated and resolute American came to my office with an idea. Her name is Helen Krieble, and she is here with us today.

Helen is the founder and president of the Vernon K. Krieble Foundation, a private foundation dedicated to public policy and America's founding principles. She is on the front lines in this debate, literally. She hires 10 guest workers each year for her business, the Colorado Horse Park, which is a major equestrian and events center in Parker, Colorado. She hires them legally, but as she can tell you, the bureaucracy is confounding.

Helen came to me with an idea. She asked why we couldn't have a no-amnesty guest worker program run by the private market instead of the government. Helen's idea represents the core of the Border Integrity and Immigration Reform Act, and I readily acknowledge that. Helen Krieble is living proof that the best ideas don't come from Washington, D.C., but come from the creative minds of men and women living the American Dream. . . .

Say No to Amnesty

We must say no to amnesty in any form. My bill offers a no-amnesty solution to the problem of 12 million illegal aliens living in our country. Some argue that there is no amnesty if these 12 million illegal aliens are required to pay a fine or back taxes. The President and many in the Senate seem to believe this to be the proper path. I disagree.

There is virtually no support back home in my district for amnesty, and let me say emphatically that this has nothing to do with race or ethnic discrimination. It has everything to do with the fundamental belief of every American in law and order. America is, and always has been, a welcoming society. This sentiment is essentially an expression of a moral principle. The ancient words from the Bible, "Do not mistreat an alien or oppress him for you were aliens in Egypt," reflect the sentiment of millions of Americans who share this compassionate view of the illegal aliens in our midst. But there still is no support back home for amnesty.

Now let's define terms. Amnesty in this context is allowing people whose first act in America was an illegal act to get right with the law without leaving the country. Allowing 12 million illegal aliens to stay in our country instead of leaving and coming back legally is amnesty, no matter if fines or back taxes are paid, or how it is otherwise dressed up or spun by its proponents. The only way to deal with these 12 million people is to insist that they leave the country and come back legally if there's a willing employer waiting in this country to put them to work.

But people ask, "Congressman, if you're not going to provide amnesty, what are you going to do with 12 million illegal aliens?"

They recognize it is not logistically possible to round up 12 million illegal aliens. When I think of the horrific images in the world press the night [young Cuban refugee] Elian Gonzalez was taken into custody, I can't imagine the American people would put up with that for very long. We know that this idea of putting everybody on buses and conducting a mass deportation is a non-starter. It also is not realistic to think that some American businesses can operate without the workers who have made their way into our economy: And it is unreasonable to think that people who came to America illegally and found jobs will voluntarily leave those jobs and opportunities without knowing whether they can return legally. . . .

A Temporary Worker Program

Private worker placement agencies that we might call Ellis Island Centers will be licensed by the federal government to match willing guest workers with jobs in America that *employers cannot fill with American workers.* U.S. employers will engage the private agencies and request guest workers. In a matter of days, the private agencies will be able to match guest workers with jobs, perform a health screening, fingerprint them and provide the appropriate information to the FBI and Homeland Security so that a background check can be performed, and provide the guest worker with a visa granted by the State Department. The visa will be issued only outside of the United States.

Outside of the United States is a key point; it is the provision that will require the 12 million illegal aliens to leave. Now, some of you are thinking to yourselves that 12 million people aren't going to pack up and leave just to get a visa to come back legally. I believe most will.

A Quick and Efficient System

The process that I just described to you will take a matter of one week or less. That is the beauty of the program. Speed is so important. No employer in America wants to lose employees for an extended amount of time. No worker who is earning money to feed and clothe a family can afford to be off the job for long.

But an employer faced with a looming requirement to verify the legality of his employees and stiff fines for employing illegal aliens will be willing to use a quick system to obtain legal employees. And an illegal alien currently employed in America will be willing to take a quick trip across the border to come back outside of the shadows and in a job where he or she does not fear a raid by Immigration and Customs Enforcement officers.

Who wouldn't take a week to do that? We are talking about people who apart from this violation of the law are for the most part staying right with the law, working hard, providing for their families, going to church on Sundays, and being good and decent people in the community. Why on earth would we assume as a nation that they wouldn't seize the opportunity to get right with the law?

In fact, I envision employers working with placement agencies to make sure that their long-time illegal employees get their paperwork, processed, background checks performed, and visas issued so that they will be back on the job quickly.

Imagine for a moment the alternative. Imagine asking millions of people to line up at the U.S. Consulate in Mexico City to obtain a visa to come to America as a guest worker. It would be a disaster. And it is precisely that image that is driving the move toward amnesty in the United States Senate. Now, imagine this. Imagine private companies competing against each other to process guest worker applicants and match the applicants with open jobs. Imagine the application of American business ingenuity to this process. That, my friends, is why this program will work. . . .

Strict Employer Enforcement

With a guest worker program in place, there is no reason why an employer ever should hire or continue to employ an illegal alien. Employers who choose to operate outside of the system, however, must face tough fines in order to be made to comply. That is what the enforcement system and the new fine structure will do.

The strict employer enforcement contained in the House-passed bill is contained in my bill. It sets forth a nationwide electronic employment verification system through which employers will verify the legality of each prospective and current employee. Right now employers are put in a no-win situation. Under the law, they must accept employees with documents that reasonably appear on their face to be genuine. It represents a violation of an individual's privacy rights to inquire further about the legitimacy of their documents. Employers cannot challenge them without risking a lawsuit. . . .

Employer enforcement is the key. Once this is in place, jobs for illegal immigrants will dry up. Why hire an illegal immigrant when you can hire a legal guest worker and eliminate the possibility of a big fine? Why stay in the country illegally when you can quickly return home and come back as a legal guest worker?

Is all of this pie in the sky? Only if you do not believe in the private market or American business. Only if you do not believe that Americans are an open-minded people with compassionate hearts. Only if you do not believe in the desire of those who are here illegally to have the opportunity to get right with the law.

Immigration Legislation Should Not Punish All Illegal Immigrants

Sen. Edward M. Kennedy

Edward M. Kennedy is a member of the United States Senate, serving the state of Massachusetts since 1962. The following statement was delivered at a field hearing of the Senate Judiciary Committee on Immigration Policy at the National Constitution Center on July 5, 2006. In his statement, Kennedy argues that spending more money on border security has not worked in the past and that a border fence would only work to further demonize undocumented workers. Kennedy makes the case for a comprehensive immigration policy that would include a route for qualified immigrants to legally come to the United States for work. He argues that immigrant workers help the U.S. economy by doing jobs that Americans would rather not do. Kennedy was a cosponsor of the Comprehensive Reform Act of 2006, which was never passed.

Two hundred thirty years and one day ago, here in Philadelphia, we declared our independence and launched a nation of freedom and opportunity that is the envy of the world. So today, as we consider immigration reform, we have a solemn duty to uphold our one nation under God, with liberty and justice for all, and to preserve and strengthen it for future generations.

The challenge before us is complex. We cannot solve it, as the House of Representatives has proposed, by simply building more fences at the border, demonizing the 12 million undocu-

Sen. Edward M. Kennedy, "Examining the Need for Comprehensive Immigration Reform," Statement Given at the National Constitution Center, July 5, 2006. Reproduced by permission of the author.

mented immigrants, declaring them and the priests and Good Samaritans who help them to be criminals, and naively hoping they just go home.

Those on the far right who continue that enforcement-only, anti-immigrant drumbeat may think it's good politics. But their pandering threatens real progress toward effective immigration reform that protects our security and reflects our values as a nation of immigrants.

We have tried it their way by simply beefing up the border. We've spent more than $20 billion on it over the past decade—and it has not worked.

It is a formula for failure that will assure continued illegal immigration and leave us weak and less secure. It disparages good, hardworking immigrant families that have come here to improve their lives and to contribute to America—some of whom serve in our armed forces and are risking their lives in Iraq and Afghanistan today.

A Comprehensive Immigration Policy

They should instead listen to President [George W.] Bush and to a bipartisan majority in the United States Senate when we came together to say that a complex problem such as immigration requires a comprehensive solution. They should listen to business leaders, religious leaders, and community leaders when we came together to pass effective reform. But most of all, they should listen to the American people who want immigration laws that not only will keep out those who would harm us, but welcome those who would help us.

The reforms we passed in the United States Senate, under the leadership of Chairman [Arlen] Specter, Senator [John] McCain and many others, started by modernizing and strengthening our enforcement. But to succeed, we knew that we must take other realistic and effective steps at the same time. Clearly we are not going to round up and deport millions of men, women, and children, or to expect that enforcement could be made so harsh, that five percent of our workforce would decide to "self-deport." So our reforms bring the 12 million undocumented immigrants who are here now out of the shadows so that they may earn the privilege of becoming taxpaying, fully-contributing citizens and members of society. And for the future, we recognize that the demand for immigrants will continue.

Therefore, we provide a way for qualified immigrants to come here legally to meet the needs of employers and our economy while protecting the wages and jobs of American citizens.

Today's hearing focuses on several important issues: whether state and local law enforcement should be in the business of enforcing federal civil immigration laws and whether immigration reform should include a new temporary worker program.

One of the most controversial and counterproductive policies the enforcement-only proponents have proposed is the use of state and local law enforcement agencies to enforce federal civil immigration laws.

I have heard strong objections from state and local officials around the country who believe such a policy will seriously hamper, and not enhance, their efforts to fight crime and protect us from future terrorist attacks. The concerns raised are shared by many conservatives and security experts— all say that this would unreasonably burden local law enforcement, irreparably damage community policing programs, impose heavy financial costs on state and local governments and jeopardize the safety our neighborhoods and diverse communities.

Most importantly, this proposal undermines our national security. Since [the terrorists attacks of] 9-11, security experts have repeatedly asserted that good intelligence is the key to ensuring national security. Ground truth comes from all sources, and often from immigrant communities. If communication shuts down because immigrants are afraid to approach local law enforcement for fear of being deported, then we lose important information and we jeopardize the security of our nation.

Immigrant Workers Help U.S. Economy

Let me turn now to the issue of immigrant workers. Some question whether immigrant workers make important contributions to the American economy. Economists tell us that the answer to that question is yes. A recent letter signed by 500 economists, including five Nobel laureates, states clearly that "immigration has been a net gain for ... American citizens," that "immigrants do not take American jobs," and that the benefits of immigration outweigh its costs. I request unanimous consent that the entire letter be added to the record.

The fact is immigrants bring job skills which complement those of workers.

It's true at the high end of the skills spectrum, where immigrants represent forty to fifty percent of graduate students in strategic fields such as engineering and the physical sciences. High-tech employers need the world's best and brightest workers to remain competitive and to create more jobs for Americans here at home.

It's also true at the low end of the skills spectrum, where employers in much of the country are unable to find U.S. workers willing and able to do needed jobs in agriculture, building maintenance, health care, and food service. These are essential jobs as America shifts from an industrial to a post-industrial economy. Eight of the fifteen occupations projected by the Labor Department to have the fastest growth in the next decade are in fields especially dependent on immigrant labor.

Conditions for Success

The Senate's guest-worker program and green card reforms will ensure that the supply of visas meets the demands of our economy. It's the most realistic step we can take to fix our broken immigration system and create the conditions for successful enforcement. And it provides greater assurance that future immigration will be within the law, instead of underground, so that immigrants are less likely to be exploited, less likely to harm American wages and jobs, and are more likely to pay taxes.

We must make sure that a temporary worker program avoids the brutal legacy of exploitation that tarnished past guest worker programs. Anything less will subject migrants to abuse and undermine the jobs, wages and working conditions of U.S. workers.

The Senate bill addresses these concerns by establishing the best temporary worker program in our nation's history:

- Temporary workers will not replace US workers. Employers may hire an immigrant only after spending 60 days attempting to recruit US workers at the prevailing wage being offered.

- Prevailing wages will be high enough to protect American workers, relying on . . . collective bargaining agreements, and Labor Department surveys.

- Foreign labor contractors will be tightly regulated; temporary workers will not be able to circumvent the law by working as independent contractors.

- Temporary workers will be able to change jobs. Employers must comply with the rules or risk losing their labor force.

- Temporary workers will be able to join unions, and cannot be hired if the company is involved in a labor dispute.

- Perhaps most important, temporary workers will have the right to adjust to permanent residence after one to four years. High-skilled workers already have this opportunity, and the same standards should apply to other immigrant workers, too.

• Finally, the bill authorizes funding for 2,000 new Labor Department inspectors. History tells us that boots-on-the-ground enforcement is essential to prevent workers from being victimized by bad apple employers who disrupt wages and working conditions.

An Opportunity to Earn Legal Status

The Senate bill also incorporates the AgJOBS [Agricultural Jobs] bill which will give farm workers and their families the dignity and justice they deserve, and give agricultural employees a legal workforce. The legislation provides a fair and reasonable way for undocumented agricultural workers to earn legal status. And it reforms the current visa program, so that employers unable to find American workers can hire needed foreign workers and workers receive the protections they deserve.

The more we consider this issue, the clearer it becomes that immigrant workers are essential for our economic security and growth, and that the Senate temporary worker program is the right way to manage their contribution and prevent undocumented employment.

Amnesty for Illegal Immigrants Is Bad for the United States

Kris W. Kobach

In the following viewpoint, Kris W. Kobach argues that, if passed, the Comprehensive Immigration Reform Act of 2006 would be a serious threat to U.S. national security. Kobach believes that the Senate bill would make life easier for terrorists to remain in the country without fear of deportation. He believes that offering a pathway to legal status will also give potential terrorists more access to move freely from country to country, making communication with terrorist states and organizations more readily available. Kobach warns Americans that this Senate bill is nothing other than amnesty for terrorists. The Comprehensive Immigration Reform Act of 2006 never won majority support in the Senate. Kris W. Kobach is a professor of law at the University of Missouri–Kansas City. He served as the U.S. attorney general's chief adviser on immigration law between 2001 and 2003.

Proponents of the Senate's comprehensive immigration bill are attempting to rhetorically recast the massive amnesty proposal as national security legislation. "It's a matter of our national security," insisted Senator Ted Kennedy (D-MA), a sponsor of the legislation. Commerce Secretary Carlos Gutierrez has echoed the point repeatedly: "This is a national security bill. We are fixing a national security problem." The legislation, proponents claim, would encourage or even compel all illegal aliens—terrorists included—to come forward and reveal their true identities as well as any criminal or terrorist connections that they may have. In reality, however, the legis-

Kris W. Kobach, "The Senate Immigration Bill: A National Security Nightmare," *Heritage Foundation*, Web Memo # 1513, July 19, 2007. Copyright © 2007 The Heritage Foundation. Reproduced by permission.

lation would actually *create* a national security problem by providing new opportunities and advantages for alien terrorists currently operating on American soil.

The Alien Terrorist Threat

The revelation of the [2007] terrorist plot to bomb JFK Airport serves as a timely reminder that alien terrorists are operating in the United States. Terrorists are busy thinking of new ways to kill innocent Americans while the Senate thinks of new ways to grant a massive amnesty to 12–20 million illegal aliens.

The four JFK terrorists [who were arrested in June 2007] include two nationals of Guyana, one of Trinidad, and one former Guyanan who was granted U.S. citizenship. The Fort Dix Islamic terrorists who were arrested in May [2007] included five foreign nationals from Yugoslavia and Jordan. A sixth, from Turkey, eventually obtained U.S. citizenship. Of the five aliens, three were illegal aliens who snuck across the southern border years ago near Brownsville, Texas.

It is a certainty that many more illegal alien terrorists are quietly at work in the United States. In fiscal year 2005, the Border Patrol apprehended 3,722 aliens from nations that are designated state sponsors of terrorism or places in which [the terrorist organization] al-Qaeda has operated, and for every one alien whom the Border Patrol apprehended, there were likely three aliens who were not caught. If so, it is probable that more than 10,000 aliens from high-risk, terrorist-associated countries illegally entered the United States in fiscal year 2005 alone. Assuming conservatively that only one in 100 was an actual terrorist, that is still over 100 terrorists who snuck across the border in a single year.

Giving Terrorists Options

Inexplicably, proponents of the Kennedy amnesty bill assume that its enactment will allow the federal government to identify these terrorists. On the contrary, the bill will make it easier for alien terrorists to operate in the United States by allowing them to create fraudulent identities with ease. To understand what will happen if the bill becomes law, assume the perspective of the illegal alien terrorist operating within the United States.

Within 180 days after the President signs the legislation, the Department of Homeland Security *must* start handing out amnesties, in the form of "probationary" Z visas. (No border security triggers need to be met; the amnesty comes first, according to Sections 1(a) and 601(f)(2) of the bill.) At that point, the terrorist can choose whichever of three options suits him best.

Terrorist Option #1

The terrorist can simply continue engaging in terrorist planning while remaining unlawfully present in the United States.

This option is particularly easy if the terrorist lives in a sanctuary city, in which the police refuse to inform the federal government when they come into contact with illegal aliens. Most major U.S. cities are now sanctuary cities, including New York City, Los Angeles, and, most recently, Detroit. Detroit's huge population of Middle Eastern immigrants provides perfect cover for newly arrived terrorists from the Middle East.

Terrorists know all about sanctuary cities and the concealment that such cities provide. The Fort Dix terrorists are a case in point. The group's three illegal aliens were pulled over a total of 19 times by local police for traffic violations. But because of sanctuary policies, they were never reported to Immigration and Customs Enforcement (ICE).

Sanctuary cities have been prohibited under federal law for more than 10 years. Nevertheless, sanctuary cities defy this federal law with impunity, because the statute does not impose any penalty on cities that adopt sanctuary policies.

Reducing the Risks for Illegals

If proponents of the Senate bill were seriously concerned about national security, they would include a provision in the bill denying federal law enforcement funds to sanctuary cities. Such a provision would quickly bring the lawbreaking cities back into line.

Moreover, even if an alien terrorist operates in a city that is *not* a sanctuary city, the bill would not impede his operations. Indeed, the Senate immigration bill will make life easier for him by reducing the risk of deportation, because the legislation transforms Immigration and Customs Enforcement (ICE) from a law enforcement agency into an amnesty distribution center.

Under Sections 601 (h)(1) and (5) of the bill, if an ICE agent apprehends any alien who appears eligible for the Z visa (in other words, just about any illegal alien), the agent cannot detain him. Instead, ICE must provide the alien a reasonable opportunity to apply for the Z visa. This stands in stark contrast to the status quo, in which ICE can place the alien in detention and immediately initiate removal proceedings.

Under the Senate amnesty bill, the terrorist suffers no such inconvenience. Instead, being discovered by ICE merely requires him to choose either option #2 or option #3.

Terrorist Option #2

Seeking amnesty under one's real name is a promising option for any terrorist who has operated completely underground during his terrorist career. This is also a likely choice for a terrorist who has been recruited into Islamic jihad only recently. Such an individual will not have a record of past terrorist activity maintained by any government.

Unfortunately, it is also a realistic option for a terrorist who is actually known by foreign governments to be involved in a terrorist organization. Under the Senate immigration bill, there is virtually no chance that the federal government will discover his terrorist connections in time. Section 601 (h)(1) of the bill allows the government only one business day to conduct a so-called background check on each applicant. If the U.S. Citizenship and Immigration Services (USCIS) adjudicator does not find any terrorist connection in time, the alien walks out of the building with a probationary Z visa on the next business day, able to work and roam the country at will.

Twenty-four-hour background checks might suffice if the government had a single, readily searchable database of all the world's terrorists, but it does not. Much of the relevant information exists only on paper, while foreign governments are the source for other data. Twenty-four hours is a terrorist's fast track.

Worse, as a practical matter, the USCIS adjudicators would not even have 24 hours if the Senate bill were passed. As the Government Accountability Office (GAO) reported in 2006, the agency is already stretched to the breaking point by the approximately 6 million applications for immigration benefits (asylum, green cards, etc.) that it receives every year. The situation is so bad that an informal "six minute rule" is in place—adjudicators are pressed to spend no more than six minutes looking at any application. The GAO concluded that failure to detect fraud is already "an ongoing and serious problem" at the agency.

Assuming (conservatively) that 12 million illegal aliens apply for the amnesty within the year allowed, it would triple the incoming workload—from 6 million applications to 18 million. Because of the 24-hour time limit, applications for the amnesty would receive only a few minutes of scrutiny. It is a certainty that applications from terrorists would be granted.

Legal Status for Terrorists

Even under the present system—in which there is no time limit on background checks—terrorists have had little difficulty in obtaining amnesties. In one case, Mahmud "the Red" Abouhalima fraudulently obtained legal status under the 1986 amnesty that was supposed to be limited to seasonal agricultural workers. He was actually driving a cab in New York City and was also a ringleader in the 1993 terrorist attacks against the World Trade Center. After receiving legal status, he traveled abroad for terrorist training. His brother Mohammed—a fellow terrorist in the plot—also obtained legal status under the 1986 amnesty.

The above examples are not isolated cases. A 2005 study by Janice Kephart, Counsel to the 9/11 Commission, found that 59 out of 94 foreign-born terrorists (about 2/3) successfully committed immigration fraud to acquire or adjust legal status.

With his newly acquired legal status, a terrorist can operate with a great deal more freedom, secure in the knowledge that a traffic violation will not lead to deportation. He can also exit and re-enter the country, allowing him greater access to international terrorist networks. The Senate immigration bill literally opens up a world of possibilities for illegal alien terrorists.

Terrorist Option #3

The third option is perhaps the most troubling. The Senate bill fails to provide any safeguards against terrorists who invent entirely "clean" identities. Because the bill contains no requirement that the alien produce a secure foreign passport proving his identity, terrorists will have little trouble gaming the system.

A terrorist can walk into a USCIS office and offer a completely fictitious name—one that does not have any negative information associated with it. In other words, a terrorist can declare that his name is "Rumpelstiltskin," or perhaps "Mohammed X," and most likely, walk out the next day with a probationary Z visa, complete with a government-issued ID card backing up his false identity.

The terrorist need only provide two easily forged pieces of paper indicating that a person of that name was in the country before January 1, 2007. A pay stub, a bank receipt, or a remittance receipt would suffice, as does a declaration from one of the terrorist's friends that he was in the country before January 1, 2007.

With this newly minted identity backed up by an ID card issued by the federal government, the alien terrorist will be armed with the perfect "breeder document," allowing him to obtain driver's licenses and just about any other form of identification that he desires. This is essentially what the 19 9/11 hijackers did: They used their passports and visas as breeder documents to obtain 63 driver's licenses. The documents allowed them to travel openly and board airplanes easily.

Congress could close this loophole relatively easily by requiring each applicant for the Z-visa amnesty to produce a secure passport with embedded biometrics. Senator Kennedy and other proponents of the bill are unlikely to fix that loophole, however. The majority of the 12–20 million illegal aliens in the United States do not possess a passport—much less a passport with embedded biometrics (which have been issued only [since 2006] by most countries). Requiring illegal aliens to present such a passport would disqualify too many aliens for the pro-amnesty crowd. The flaw exposes what a deception the "national security" claim is.

Amnesty for Terrorists

Supporters of the Senate's comprehensive immigration reform bill have revived it under the guise of national security. However, the new public relations campaign is a farce. The bill offers alien terrorists new pathways to obtain legal status, which will make it easier for them to carry out deadly attacks against American citizens.

The top priority in this bill is extending amnesty as quickly and easily as possible to as many illegal aliens as possible. The cost of doing so is to jeopardize national security.

Amnesty for Illegal Immigrants Is Good for the United States

Justin Akers Chacon

Justin Akers Chacon maintains in the following viewpoint that the only individuals making the argument for the amnesty of illegal immigrants are ordinary citizens. He contends that the argument for amnesty is absent from the halls of Congress. Chacon views the political debate as being between "enforcement" Republicans, who believe any guest-worker program is identical to amnesty, and "guest-worker" Republicans and Democrats, who are helping big business by making it easier for corporate America to continue to offer immigrant workers low wages. He maintains that the guest-worker proposals in Congress are meant to stifle the organized labor movement. Chacon argues that the political debate needs to be broadened to include amnesty and legalization but that this will only happen if ordinary citizens organize and demand change. Justin Akers Chacon is a professor of U.S. history and Chicano studies in San Diego, California. He is also the coauthor of No One Is Illegal: Fighting Violence and State Repression on the U.S.-Mexico Border *(2006).*

A specter is haunting Congress—the specter of amnesty. As millions of immigrant workers and students strike, walk out and protest against anti-immigrant legislation being discussed in Congress, the debate over amnesty is beginning.

Taking place primarily as a fight within the Republican Party, amnesty is becoming the subtext for a polarization in the politics of immigration. Only no one in Washington is supporting it.

On one side are the "enforcement" Republicans, critical of any guest-worker proposals since they contain language about

Justin Akers Chacon, "The Case for Amnesty," *Socialist Worker Online*, April 7, 2007. Reproduced by permission.

a "pathway to citizenship." Appealing to their conservative base to halt the march of immigrant rights, the "enforcement" Republicans pander to fears, insecurities and outright racism.

As Senate Majority Leader Bill Frist (R-Tenn.) complained, "I disagree with [guest-worker proposals] not just as a matter of principle, but because granting amnesty now will only encourage future and further disrespect for the law. It will undermine our efforts to secure our homeland."

Anyone who supports such proposals, said Rep. Steve King (R-Iowa), should be "branded with a scarlet letter A," for "amnesty."

According to Rep. Tom Tancredo (R-Colo.), a darling of the hard-line right-wing anti-immigrant organizations who launched his congressional career in 1998 on a platform of opposition to amnesty, immigrants are "a scourge that threatens the very future of our nation." Tancredo followed his latest tirade with a "Just Say No to Amnesty Week" campaign, urging supporters to turn the screws on Republican senators who are "selling out America" by supporting more moderate immigration legislation that includes plans for a guest-worker program.

Guest-Worker Politics

On another side of the debate are the "guest-worker" Republicans and Democrats, eager to secure cheap labor for big business. They are determined to prove that the guest-worker proposals are *not* an amnesty, but rather a means to prevent one.

Referring to his own guest-worker proposal, Arizona Sen. John McCain explained that it focused on enforcement. In a statement on the Web site of Sen. Ted Kennedy (D-Mass.), who cosponsored the bill McCain supports, McCain stated, "Homeland security is our nation's number one priority. This legislation includes a number of provisions that together will make our nation more secure. For far too long, our nation's broken immigration laws have gone unreformed—leaving

Americans vulnerable. We can no longer afford to delay reform. I am proud to join my colleagues today as an original sponsor of this legislation."

Sen. Arlen Specter (R-Pa.), who has entered the picture as a broker trying to reconcile the "enforcement" and "guest-worker" wings in Congress, has also come out firmly against amnesty. Promoting a recent compromise proposal that increases border militarization and includes a guest-worker proposal, Specter declared, "It is not an amnesty." In an amnesty, he told the *Los Angeles Times*, "lawbreakers do not have to pay for their transgressions."

Kennedy likewise assured his colleagues, "There is no free Ticket. . . . This is not amnesty."

A New Civil Rights Movement

There is a third side to the debate, and though it isn't recognized as an "official" voice, it is now shifting the terms of the debate. That side is the U.S. working class, led by millions of immigrant workers, their children and their supporters.

The [spring 2006] mass protests and student walkouts have shaken the country. This new civil rights movement has shifted the debate about immigration out of the executive boardrooms, golf clubs and annual stockholder meetings, and forced it into the open.

The movement is putting pressure on Congress to come up with a "plan B" to the Sensenbrenner Bill passed [in] December [2005] by the House, which embodies the program of the "enforcement" Republicans.

Republican House Speaker Dennis Hastert summed up the new common ground. "Our first priority is to protect the border," Hastert said. "And we also know there is a need in some sectors of the economy for a guest-worker program. But we want to see what the Senate comes forward with, and we will go through the process."

Workers Without Rights

There are two reasons why a guest-worker program is emerging as the bipartisan consensus in Washington.

Guest-worker programs, by their very nature, create a second class of workers in the U.S. Current proposals would allow workers to remain in the country for a limited duration, after which they must leave or compete for a scarce number of visas.

While in this country, guest workers don't have the rights afforded to other workers. They aren't allowed to collectively bargain, join unions or speak out against exploitative bosses, and can only leave an oppressive job if they have another already lined up.

This is why [Chicano activist] Cesar Chavez and the United Farm Workers could only build the historic farmworker struggle after winning the abolition of the last guest-worker program, known as the bracero program, in 1964.

Under the bracero program, growers were able to turn agriculture into a $40 billion-a-year industry by keeping out unions and setting a standard for low wages. The legacy, according to a study by the *Sacramento Bee*, is that the many poor farmworkers make no more that $4,000 a year today.

As labor journalist David Bacon concluded, guest-worker "proposals incorporate demands by the Essential Worker Immigration Coalition—36 of the U.S.'s largest trade and manufacturers' associations, headed by the U.S. Chamber of Commerce. . . . Despite their claims, there is no great shortage of workers in the U.S. There is a shortage of workers at the low wages industry would like to pay."

The Suppression of Organized Labor

The guest-worker proposals are designed to prevent or reduce unionism in industries beyond agriculture. Current proposals, embraced by a host of corporate interests, would allow guest workers to be used in construction, meatpacking, hotels and restaurants, manufacturing, transportation, health care and other sectors of the economy.

It is within these very industries that immigrant workers have played a key role revitalizing the union movement in the last two decades. While union membership has been declining over the last three decades, immigrant workers are a growth engine.

According to a study of the Migrant Policy Institute, 11 percent of the 17.7 million foreign-born workers in the U.S. are represented by unions, despite the difficulties associated with citizenship. Reflecting changing attitudes in the unions and militancy among immigrant workers themselves, the number of immigrants in unions has grown 23 percent between 1996 and 2003.

The Service Employees Industrial Union (SEIU), with members primarily in property services, health care and the public sector, has become the largest and fastest growing union in the U.S., claiming a membership of 1.8 million. Immigrant workers account for some two-thirds of that figure.

A new guest-worker program would halt union growth in those sectors and trigger a gradual erosion as braceros could be used as leverage against union drives and contract negotiations. A new guest-worker program would create a vast segregated workforce, controlled and exploited by big business— and set the workers' movement back to the days before Cesar Chavez and the farmworkers' movement.

A New Amnesty

An amnesty is a provision that allows for the immediate legalization of the undocumented, with a guaranteed means of attaining citizenship for those who want it. Unlike current proposals, which use the deceptive language of "earned" citizenship or a "path to" citizenship and which exclude the majority from obtaining permanent residency, amnesty would make immigrants equals with the rest of the working class.

The last amnesty, passed in 1986, led to legalization and citizenship for about 2.8 million immigrant workers. This set the stage for a new generation of organizing drives that fed unions like the SEIU, UNITE-HERE and others.

While other unions were pushed on the defensive, immigrant worker-led union drives demonstrated a willingness to fight. This led the AFL-CIO [American Federation of Labor and Congress of Industrial Organizations] to support the organizing of immigrants, including the undocumented, and led to a growing demand amongst workers themselves for a new amnesty.

This is the demand now emanating from the streets, and it is sending chills down the spine of Corporate America.

Organize to Demand Legalization

If the 11 million undocumented workers in the U.S. today [2006] were given equal rights, it would abolish the legal segregation that serves as the means to exploit the powerless. It would also undermine the racism that justifies the militarization of the border. It would give a voice to the voiceless and increase the number of voters who could have recourse against politicians trying to build their careers by scapegoating immigrants. It would also help revitalize a labor movement in crisis.

As the new immigrant rights movement awakens, it must put forth its own proposal: Amnesty without criminalization. As Maria Gonzalez, a marcher at the demonstration of 1 million in Los Angeles March 25, [2006,] commented as she considered the masses of workers around her, "With this many people, we should demand legalization and amnesty."

While Congress is being forced to respond to the demands of the protests, it is only as a means to defend corporate interests, reshuffle their cards and head off a new civil rights move ment. Only when the politicians are forced to concede to the organized power of a united movement will they reluctantly accept our demands.

That is why we must continue to build the immigrant rights movement, independent of the bipartisan legislative proposals that serve Corporate America. We have to organize where we have the most power: in the workplaces, schools and communities.

State Governments Are Forced to Act in the Absence of Federal Immigration Reform

T.R. Reid

T.R. Reid is the Rocky Mountain bureau chief for the Washington Post. *He is also a commentator for National Public Radio and the author of five books, including* The United States of Europe: The New Superpower and the End of American Supremacy. *In the following article, Reid reports that state lawmakers from across the country are proposing legislation to reform illegal immigration in their respective states. Reid contends that many of these lawmakers are acting out of frustration, shared by many constituents, regarding the inability of the U.S. Congress to agree on immigration legislation. Among the reasons for this sense of legislative urgency are the unusually high numbers of immigrants entering the country illegally and the anxiety many Americans feel about having an insecure border. Although some lawmakers agree that a multistate approach to curbing immigration is not ideal, they feel that federal inaction has left them no other option.*

State legislatures around the nation are considering hundreds of proposals dealing with illegal immigration, reflecting the exasperation of many local officials with Congress's failure to contend with the millions of undocumented workers who have entered the nation in recent years.

Here in Arizona, the House has passed a proposal to set fines and other penalties for companies that hire undocumented workers. The bill, which had regularly failed in previous years, is expected to win Senate approval . . . and is only one of many plans under consideration.

Others include bills to erect an 80-mile fence and a multimillion-dollar radar system along the Mexican border, designed to slow the nightly flow of migrants across the desert. Another bill would require police to check the citizenship of anyone stopped for a traffic offense. The state House, by a vote of 43 to 12, has passed a resolution calling on Washington to dispatch the U.S. Coast Guard to this landlocked, coast-free state to assist in patrolling the border.

A Multistate Approach

For the most part, the new state measures are designed to get tough on illegal immigrants, on employers who give them jobs and on state officials who give them benefits. In some states, illegal immigrants can buy lottery tickets but cannot collect if they win a significant prize.

At the same time, though, some states are moving in the other direction—making life easier for immigrants, legal or otherwise. In April [2006], Nebraska's legislature overrode a gubernatorial veto to offer in-state college tuition rates to the children of illegal immigrants. Nine other states have formally authorized tuition breaks for undocumented immigrants, and many public universities employ a "don't ask, don't tell" policy for graduates of high schools in the states.

Maryland and Virginia lawmakers considered proposals to crack down on illegal immigrants in their concluded legislative sessions, but none passed.

The multistate approach, with some states at variance with others, threatens to create a maze of laws and regulations at a time when the nation as a whole is struggling with how to contend with an unprecedented wave of illegal immigration.

"We're not going to solve this problem with a patchwork approach at the state level. It's a national problem, and the need is to repair the national system," said Josh Bernstein of the National Immigration Law Center, which works to promote the rights of low-income immigrants. "We're not going to erect barriers between states."

Advocates on both sides said that [the] economic boycott and rallies [on May 1, 2006,] will work to their advantage. Opponents of illegal immigration said the protests hardened their resolve, while immigrants' rights activists predicted that the large turnout will sway lawmakers to their side.

Frustrated by Federal Inaction

The National Conference of State Legislatures [NCSL] has tallied 463 bills introduced [in 2006] in 43 states, by far the biggest crop of state immigration proposals ever recorded. Ann Morse, who tracks the issue for the NCSL, said this rush of legislation demonstrates that state legislators are no longer willing to cede this high-profile political concern to Congress.

Morse cited three reasons for the unprecedented interest in immigration at the state level. "First, there's the reaction to 9/11 and the concern that our borders are not safe," she said. "Another factor is the number of immigrants and a general sense that the influx is growing rapidly. And finally, we seem to have a Congress in gridlock on the issue. State legislators feel if they don't act, nobody will."

That last concern has been crucial in the legislature [in Arizona], noted state Rep. Russell K. Pearce, a Republican who says he is "fed up" with his own party's management of the issue in Washington.

"We had high hopes that Congress would do something [in 2006]," Pearce said. "But Washington is ducking its responsibility. Our constituents are outraged about that. So they are demanding—and I mean demanding—that we do the job instead."

With opinion surveys showing intense public concern about immigration [in 2006], Congress has been sharply divided. The House passed a tough anti-immigration bill that included stiff criminal measures and costly new efforts in border control. In the Senate, many lawmakers favor a guest-worker program and finding a way to allow some illegal immigrants to seek citizenship. So far, however, the legislation has been mired in committee.

With the two houses seeming to be on divergent paths, state officials are losing hope for federal immigration initiatives [in 2006]. "If Congress were able to act, there would be much less activity in the state legislatures," Bernstein said.

Utilizing State Resources

The most common approach to immigration at the state level [in 2006], the NCSL tally shows, is criminal legislation to impose sanctions on employers who knowingly hire illegal immigrants. More than half the states are considering employment legislation in various forms, and many bills are expected to pass.

On April 17, [2006] Georgia Gov. Sonny Perdue (R) signed a law that imposes fines on employers of undocumented workers and requires any company with a state contract to fire any employee who is not a legal resident. The Georgia law also requires that state offices verify an employee's status before paying unemployment benefits or workers' compensation. Similar provisions are found in pending bills in several other states.

Legislatures in Ohio, South Dakota and Arizona have passed bills [in 2006] requiring that state or local police check the immigration status of everybody they encounter, and report suspected illegal immigrants to U.S. Immigration and Customs Enforcement. Several other states have similar bills pending.

Many police chiefs and mayors oppose this approach, fearing that immigrants will be frightened to contact the police when they need help. But proponents say that the initial police contact is the best time to catch somebody who should not be here. As Pearce puts it, "Deportation should start with the traffic stop."

More than a dozen states are considering legislation that would require proof of citizenship or of legal-resident status for anybody seeking a driver's license. Some would simply deny illegal immigrants the right to drive. Other proposals are similar to a bill that passed in Utah [in 2005], offering undocumented applicants only a "driving privilege" certificate that is not supposed to be treated as legal identification. Virginia requires license applicants to offer proof of legal status.

There are also bills pending in several state capitols to help undocumented workers deal with the problems that come with their status. Several states seek to get tough on "notarios," people without a law degree who sell costly "consulting" services to immigrants seeking legal-residence status or citizenship. Some state governments help employers fill out the I-9 form that is required for immigrant workers under federal law.

One State's Response

Polls show that immigration is considered a bigger problem in Arizona than gasoline prices. Republican Sen. Jon Kyl and Jim Pederson, his Democratic challenger, are already saturating the airwaves for the [2006] election—and the ads deal mainly with immigration.

[In 2006], the Republican-controlled legislature has passed several bills designed to crack down on illegal immigration; Democratic Gov. Janet Napolitano has vetoed several of them. Pearce, sponsor of the employer-crackdown legislation, said the anti-illegal-immigration majority in the legislature plans to package all the measures into a comprehensive bill. That would set up a new confrontation with the governor.

The bill that seems most likely to become law here [in 2006] is Pearce's employer-sanction plan. Napolitano said in

January [2006] that she would sign an employer-sanction bill. Even business groups concede that approval is likely.

"Our position has been that employment of immigrants is a federal issue, and it deserves a federal response," said Farrell Quinlan of the Arizona Chamber of Commerce and Industry. "But if the federal government doesn't act, you're going to see the states try to fill the void."

CHAPTER 4

Personal Perspectives
on Illegal Immigration

My Family's Journey Across the U.S. Border

Faviola Rubio

In the following personal account, Faviola Rubio relates some of the hardships her family faced while crossing the U.S.-Mexico border into the United States. She recounts the story of how her father carried his brother on his back after he had collapsed from exhaustion in the desert. Rubio also shares the story of how she and her brother were drugged and brought across the border in the trunk of a car and tells of the many sacrifices that her mother made in the hope of making a better life for her children in the United States. She also addresses some of the obstacles immigrants face as they try to become productive members of their new country. Faviola Rubio was a student at the University of Virginia at the time she wrote this 2005 account.

A trip to the United States isn't as easy as flying down to Cancun or traveling to Europe. When visas are hard or impossible to obtain, immigrants will find other means to battle for survival and for a better future.

The first "border crossing" story in my family comes from my father and two uncles, who entered the United States through the Mexican border. First, my father and uncles had to hire a "good" coyote, a person who makes a living by transporting illegal immigrants into the United States. It costs a lot of money to hire a good coyote—about $1,000 then, and now [in 2005] $10,000. For a resident of a Latin American country, this is not an easy sum to obtain; my father made $5,000 in a year. To come up with the money, he sold his belongings and borrowed money from relatives and banks in Bolivia.

Having paid the coyote, they set off. My uncle Oscar recounted the journey: "During the night, we went through

Faviola Rubio, "A Trying Journey," The *Cavalier Daily*, April 25, 2005. Copyright © 1995–2007 The *Cavalier Daily*. Reproduced by permission.

tunnels, ran without stopping, swam through a river and climbed fences. There was a point while we were in the desert where I could not make it. I just could not move my legs anymore. I will never forget what your father did for me. He picked me up, put me on his back and continued running."

The coyotes will often leave people and continue guiding the rest of the group. In Oscar's case, the coyote wanted to leave him, but my father picked him up and ran with him on his back. Once in the United States, life was not easy, but they continued to work to send money back home to our family.

Sadly, others' stories do not end as well.

The Danger in Crossing the Border

My uncle Jose remembers running in the desert with a particular group of people, including a lady with her baby. The baby cried continuously and would not stop. So the coyote told the lady that if she did not leave the baby there in the desert, then she would have to stay behind because it was a risk for the larger group. In a state of panic, the woman left her baby. No one knows what happened to the baby. My uncle still has restless nights because of the fact that he did not oppose leaving the baby behind and did not offer to carry the baby himself. With family and unity so important in our lives, I imagine the mother and the incredible sadness she must have faced afterwards and possibly to this day.

I also came through the border my first time to the United States when I was six years old. My mom says that they had to pay extra money to have a white couple take us in their trunk. My brother and I were intoxicated and put to sleep so that we would not make any noise. My mom had to run across the border and meet us at a designated place that the coyote had set up. She said that when she saw us, we could hardly walk. She screamed at the coyote, saying, "What did you do to my children?" Once in the United States, we experienced segregation and discrimination in our new community, even from our own cousins.

Now that we are citizens of the United States, it is hard for me to see clips of others who, just like us, are trying to come to the place of opportunity for their families. To see them mistreated and beat up by border police makes me feel unsafe to even write my story. Univision and Telemundo are two Spanish channels shown in the United States that have news around 6:30 p.m. I remember I saw a clip of illegal immigrants getting off a truck and being frantically beaten by the border police. I could not eat my dinner. What happened to human rights? How can the world's "promoter of human rights" treat human beings as though they are animals?

A Mother's Sacrifice

So much of my early life is a blur. I sometimes wonder why I have blocked out some of these memories. In hopes of understanding my past, I asked my mom to tell me of our early struggles.

I come from a family that is neither among the rich nor the poor. Before we left for the United States, my mother was going through a divorce with my biological father, had two children and had just finished medical school at La Universidad San Simon in Cochabamba, Bolivia.

She set up her clinic in the countryside—where she had the only clinic within a five-mile radius. She felt needed in the community because the residents were not obtaining immediate medical care for serious injuries. She obviously did not do her work for the money because most residents could only pay with eggs, chickens or personal possessions.

My mom was about to begin studying for her specialty as a pediatrician, when she made a life-changing choice to come to the United States. She chose to leave a community where she was needed and was making a positive difference to face a situation in the United States where she struggled to simply survive. She chose this difficult reality for the sake of my brother and me, so that her children could have a better future.

The Hope for a Better Life

Many parents come to the unknown with a selfless wish for their children to have better lives than they have had and, as a result, are forced to put their own dreams behind them. As a single mother, this was exactly what my mom did. Dr. Mabel Cespedes in Bolivia, she left behind her position of power and prestige for a very different life. Since the time she entered the United States, she has never again enjoyed the rights or privileges of her education, or been referred to with the title of respect conferred to a doctor. Instead, she has been categorized and labeled as immigrant, alien and uneducated because of the work she was forced to accept.

When we first arrived in the United States, my mom cleaned hotels from 8 a.m until 5 p.m. Then she would work from 9 p.m. to 5 a.m. taking care of an elderly couple. My brother, who was in kindergarten, would walk to school by himself because my mom was at work. I was two years younger than my brother and did not have a place to stay, so I would go with my mom to clean hotels. I would hide so that the managers would not see me helping my mom—if they found out I was there, she would get fired. I would pull a little bucket of water across the hallway into the hotel rooms when no one was watching, as well as make beds and dust the furniture.

At this early point in our American residency, my mother, being a single woman with two children and little but not enough knowledge of English, was unable to take the Boards exam to get into medical school in the United States. Incredibly talented people from around the world come to the United States and encounter a system that blocks their contribution to our society.

I have noticed that many people in the United States and at this University overlook the struggles that families have gone through and the many sacrifices they make along the way in becoming productive citizens of this country. For many, including myself, my family stressed the importance of education. Their dream was to have their children become professionals who earn a place in society where they are respected and can have a positive impact for those who have no voice.

Life as an Illegal Immigrant in America

Teresa Mendez

In this selection, Teresa Mendez gives us the story of a family journey from Ciudad Juarez, a Mexican border city, to Washington's verdant Yakima Valley. She tells the story of the family's struggle to find work for her husband, Armando, and educational opportunities for their five children. Marie and her children are American citizens, but Armando is an illegal immigrant in the United States. Marie and Armando work hard and make sacrifices so that their children will have the opportunities of a good education and a better life as American citizens. Teresa Mendez is a staff writer for the Christian Science Monitor.

Twice her family has made the journey from Ciudad Juarez, on the Mexican border, through Texas, New Mexico, Arizona, Nevada, and Oregon, to settle in eastern Washington's verdant Yakima Valley.

The first time, back in 2001, they came so Marie's husband, a migrant farm worker, could harvest hops—the bitter plants used to make beer. [In 2004] they came again looking for work. And in this town of 8,000, nestled in the foothills of the Cascade Mountains, they began picking apples.

It took five days for the family of seven—Marie, her husband, Armando, and their five children—to reach Grandview. They'd planned to drive straight through, but ran out of money along the way. Each night, they slept together in their silver minivan.

A Long Journey for a Better Life

Now they describe it is an adventure: Christina, the oldest, dubbed the van their "five-star hotel." Marie remembers glimpsing the Hoover Dam. Press just a little, though, and Marie will admit that enduring a trip of more than 1,500 miles, even twice, has been two times too many for both her and her children.

It's a passage that hundreds of thousands of migrant families make round-trip year after year. Armando is just one of more than a million farm workers who move as crops ripen and seasons turn.

But for Marie, *ya basta*. Enough. "I don't plan on moving no more," she says, her round face turning uncharacteristically somber. "My kids suffered the most, and that's not fair."

Marie completed elementary and high school in the small Texas town where she was born. She hopes to give her children the same opportunity.

Because Armando is an illegal immigrant, he and Marie asked that their last names not be used in this article. About half of the country's migrant farm workers are undocumented. Marie and four of their children are US citizens.

Migrant Students

Children of migrant farm workers like Christina, Jorge, Raul, Mickaela, and Juana occupy a shadowy place in the education landscape. As they slip between schools and states their progress—and setbacks—are extremely difficult to gauge.

"Migrant kids are often the forgotten kids," says Roger Rosenthal, executive director of the Migrant Legal Action Program in Washington, D.C., who for more than 25 years has worked as an advocate for migrant children.

They have been called an "invisible minority." Hard to identify, obscured within another struggling yet more prominent demographic—impoverished Latinos—migrant students face the same obstacles as other low-income minority children. According to the Labor Department's National Agricultural Workers Survey, their families earn less than $10,000 a year. On average, farm workers have six years of formal education. Most don't speak English.

But migrants must also grapple with farm injuries and pesticide exposure; juggle school work with field work; and learn to navigate a world that is constantly in motion. With each interruption to their schooling, they risk falling behind. Just one move can increase the likelihood that a student will drop out or repeat a grade, studies show.

In his 1960 documentary "Harvest of Shame," chronicling the plight of migrant workers, [journalist] Edward R. Murrow suggested that the US government was better at counting migratory birds than migrant farm workers. It's an aphorism that applies to migrant students as well. Data on everything from their numbers to dropout and graduation rates are often rough, or culled from antiquated research.

"They're a subpopulation that really isn't studied because they're a marginalized population," says Roberto Treviño, a professor at the University of North Texas in Denton, whose research focuses on achievement in low-income Latino students. "They're off on the fringes."

An American Education

With states now required by federal law to track and report how historically ignored groups of students—including migrants—fare in such areas as reading and math, this is sure to change. But will it also translate to a fuller education for America's nearly 900,000 migrant students? While schools may be taking more note of the migrants in their midst, the same laws that require better tracking urge tougher academic standards—without necessarily creating additional support for a vulnerable group already struggling to keep up.

It's a sunny day in Grandview, crisp and pleasant. Bright wooden cutouts of fruit lining the main drag hint at just how entwined this town's identity is with agriculture. A faint smell of manure wafts through the streets.

In the fall, Marie and Armando's five children were spread between three schools. Grandview has six schools serving about 3,000 students, 550 of whom are migrant.

By many measures, they are adjusting well. Christina's transition into ninth grade has been smooth. In a room redolent of melting butter, her home economics teacher notes that the entire freshman class is, after all, new to Grandview High School. Besides, the faculty and students are familiar with families cycling in and out.

Jorge—the family "inventor"—is thriving in sixth-grade science. On this Tuesday, he's the first to connect a battery, compass, and light bulb to test electromagnetic strength.

Raul's second-grade teacher feels comfortable seating him at the back of the room. He's "a strong student," she says, able to concentrate through rows of distractions.

At recess, Mickaela twirls a jump-rope as a gaggle of second-grade girls, ponytails flying, runs through.

And Juana, liquid eyes framed by wispy strands of dark hair escaped from her braid, shyly professes to love homework. She blends easily with her classmates at Smith Elementary, where fair-haired children are in the minority. In her dual-language first-grade class—the morning is conducted in English, the afternoon in Spanish—one blond boy sticks out in a sea of dark heads.

But there's a murkier side, too.

A Lack of Stability Between Home and School

Becky Knott, her teacher, says that Juana rarely takes assignments home, and they don't always make it back. During her 15 years in Grandview, Mrs. Knott has seen countless migrant students filter through, many of whom, even at that young age, "come in low because they haven't been in one place long enough to learn anything." But with a supportive family and school, she says, they often "just zoom—they excel."

Mickaela and Raul are pulled out of class daily for ESL [English as a Second Language] lessons.

And at 8:40 every morning, Jorge joins a reading class for special-education students. Though he is clearly at the top of his class, impatient as his classmates struggle to sound out words—rugs, pop, stop, swimming—whispering answers to Sergio on his right, he reads at a first-grade level.

Twenty-four percent of the district's migrant students are a year behind grade level; 2 percent are two or more years behind, according to the state's Migrant Student Data and Recruitment Office. The 44,000 migrant students statewide are performing at about the same level.

Forty years have passed since the federal government, as part of President [Lyndon B.] Johnson's Great Society program, promised to educate all children. The Migrant Education Program was created in 1966, at a time when just 1 in 10 migrant students finished high school. In the '80s, graduation rates reached about 50 percent—still one of the lowest for any group—where they hover today. President [George W.] Bush signed the No Child Left Behind Act (NCLB) in 2002, reauthorizing Johnson's education law and reaffirming a commitment to all students, with a special pledge to poor and minority families.

And in places with year-round growing seasons, where rows of crops have long abutted school buildings, many districts are successfully addressing migrant students' needs. Even tiny Montana, with just 1,600 migrants, is held up as an example. But in other states, where their presence may be newer, or where fewer trickle through each year, many migrant students linger in the shadows.

Educators say that the goal of NCLB, to shine a light on subgroups such as "migrant" by scrutinizing their progress and holding districts and states accountable for their performance, is laudable. But, as with the law more broadly, it's the implementation that has drawn concern.

The Cost for Education

For one, as the migrant student population has grown over the past decade and costly computer technology has proven one of the most effective ways to support them, federal funding rose modestly—and actually decreased slightly to $393 million in 2004. "You have more kids and you're getting whacked by the inflation rate," says Richard Gómez Jr., president of the National Association of State Directors of Migrant Education and director of Washington's Migrant Education Program, which saw its migrant students increase by 10 percent.

Another fear is what a battery of high-stakes assessments, with more states requiring graduation exit exams, may do to an already fragile group of students. And for the roughly 50 percent who graduate, there's the looming question of how to pay for college. The cost can be prohibitive on a family's subsistence wages, and those who are not citizens might not qualify for loans or state tuition.

Helping Migrant Children and Their Families

But the biggest challenge in serving migrant students has been keeping track of them. The federal Migrant Student Records Transfer System, founded in 1969, was considered a great achievement. Besides housing health and education records, it was credited with bigger feats, like ending measles outbreaks in migrant camps. In 1994, the system was abandoned and replaced by a web of state-run programs. Now, the Education Department is looking into ways to help states link their systems, and plans to have the Migrant Student Information Exchange in place within the next few years. But it may never be as wide-reaching as a centralized federal database.

Grandview became the state's first migrant education program in 1962. Today, Yolanda Magañas, the district's migrant-home visitor, serves more than 500 families. It was she who discovered Marie's family living in an abandoned camper, cooking and bathing at a nearby labor camp. The three-bedroom single-wide, set in the Granvilla Mobile Court, where Marie's family now lives, is an immeasurable improvement.

"We have a house," says Christina. "Like a 'house,' house. There's nothing missing for us here." At dusk, Armando, in cowboy boots and a baseball cap embroidered with the Virgin of Guadalupe, ducks outside to switch on a row of twinkly blue Christmas lights.

Ms. Magañas helped them find their new home and registered the children in the Migrant Education Program. Warm, with well-coiffed dark hair, she's lived in the Yakima Valley most of her life. Her parents were migrants from Texas.

Much of the credit for improving migrant students' lives belongs to people like Magañas, advocates and educators— many once migrants themselves—who truly grasp their needs. But beyond understanding the struggle and the stigma of farm work, beyond acting as translators between families and schools, they recognize the dignity and lessons of the migrant experience.

Families Working Together

"These are powerful people," says Cinthia Salinas, a professor at the University of Texas, Austin, and editor of "Scholars in the Field: The Challenges of Migrant Education." "They coalesce around their family and their language. They take great pride in what they do."

Marie's family arrived in Grandview to orchards thick with fruit. For the few months before school started, the children climbed apple and pear trees to help their father. Though they grew tired and their hands cold, Raul and Jorge say it was fun—an adventure like their drive from Mexico.

But work dried up mid-December. For Armando this meant a sojourn in Nevada. Marie, resolute in her decision to stay, remained behind with their children.

Kevin Chase, superintendent of the Grandview School District, has witnessed 30 years of change in the Yakima Valley. There was a time when schools hired as many as five extra teachers to meet the spring influx of migrants—so many students, he says, they practically had their own school. Classes started as late as 10 a.m.—"asparagus time" to accommodate farm work. Today there is less turnover each year, as families hoping for a steadier life for their children try to eke out a living here year round.

Like parents everywhere, Armando dreams of more for Christina, Jorge, Raul, Mickaela, and Juana. He wants them to finish high school, a luxury he never had. And one day, he says in Spanish, "I hope they have careers and are able to do better than I have, working in the fields."

Patrolling the U.S. Border

Malia Politzer

In the following article, Malia Politzer goes on patrol with U.S. border agent Elizier Vasquez. Vasquez and Politzer encounter a group of Mexicans illegally crossing the Arizona border in Nogales, a border town popular for illegal crossing. This particular group of illegal immigrants had been traveling for three days and had suffered extreme conditions to reach the desert of Nogales. In their encounter with the illegal immigrants, Politzer shows how otherwise sympathetic people still need to be treated within the law. Politzer also reports that the Tucson sector of the Border Patrol faces an uphill battle to prevent illegal border-crossers. They are asked to guard 262 miles of border, most of which is open territory. This challenge is made more apparent by the fact that, even after being caught, many illegal immigrants make another attempt to cross the U.S.-Mexico border. Malia Politzer is a writer and as of 2007 was producing a documentary on illegal immigration.

Border patrol agent Elizier Vasquez gets out of his car on Elephants Head Road, a smear of dirt and gravel wedged between two slices of desert. His eyes comb the rust-colored Arizona dirt that stretches for miles to the north, south, and west, its stark beauty marred by scattered piles of trash. A few miles to the east of us is [Highway] I-19, which shoots straight from Nogales to Tucson, and past that there's more desert. We came here from the U.S.-Mexico border, about 25 miles to the south. The drive took less than 30 minutes. Walking, Vasquez tells me, would have taken about three days.

"Look at all the trash left by illegal aliens," he says, navigating through a knee-high pile of old clothes. I trip on a dusty sweatshirt; it catches in the branch of a mesquite tree and rips, brittle and weathered. Empty water jugs lie beneath the desert shrubs, the plastic brittle and broken from the heat. We navigate through backpacks, clothes, empty tuna cans. Shoes, some with soles worn out, lie in piles among the tangles of cactus and mesquite.

"We call these lay-up spots," Vasquez says in a low voice. "Illegal aliens rest here while they wait for their rides. Most are known spots. Probably we'll find the illegals sleeping under a tree. If not, they've probably already been picked up by their smugglers."

A Cat-and-Mouse Game

Lay-up spots are scattered throughout the desert along the many paths worn by the feet of illegal entrants, hundreds of sad little Ellis Islands baking under the Arizona sun. Migrants rest and clean up there, dumping everything left over from their three-day hike to rot in the desert. The spots started showing up in Arizona around 1999, after a crackdown in border towns steered those who wanted to enter the United States illegally toward the open desert.

Patrolling lay-ups is pointless. As soon as smugglers get wind that agents are watching one, they'll bring their charges to another spot a few miles down the road. It's an endless game of cat and mouse.

It's the game Vasquez lives for—though he doesn't always love it. Originally from Puerto Rico, the agent worked as a rum salesman before joining the Border Patrol in 2000 to pursue a childhood dream. "I wanted to go into law enforcement," he explained to me earlier in the day. "You know the cliché´ that little boys either want to be firemen or policemen—I never grew out of that." He and his wife moved to Arizona to pursue a new future, leaving behind everything they'd ever known.

Some days it's good. The days he apprehends aliens who are actual criminals are the best, Vasquez says, because those days he knows he's made things a little better. Even so, he admits he thinks it's unlikely the Border Patrol will ever fully control the border. "We can get operational control," he says. "We can control it to a certain point, but due to the terrain it's almost impossible to seal it off to all illegal activity."

And some days aren't so good. Like when he comes upon women with infants trying to cross the region aptly nicknamed "the death corridor."

A Life-and-Death Struggle

Welcome to the Arizona desert, where smugglers and the Border Patrol are locked in a daily struggle. One group looks for clever ways to smuggle goods and people across the border; the other looks for cleverer ways to stop them. Caught in between are the migrants, for whom the outcome can mean the difference between life and death.

Vasquez is trying to teach me the rules, but the game's already over. The Border Patrol lost a long time ago.

"We don't have any specifics on the call, so we don't know who we might run into here," Vasquez whispers as he pushes past the spiny black branches of a mesquite tree. "Could be a group of U.S. citizens out on a hike. Could be a group of drug-smuggling aliens. Could be a group of aliens in distress. We don't know, so we have to be careful."

The Risks of Patrolling

A Tucson-sector Border Patrol public relations officer, Jesus "Chuy" Rodriguez, later tells me that of all federal agents, members of the Border Patrol are the most likely to die in the line of duty. The claim is hard to substantiate, but it's certainly true that border violence has risen sharply in recent years. Attacks on agents more than doubled between 2004 and 2005, from 374 to 778, according to congressional testimony by U.S. Customs and Border Protection Commissioner T.J. Bonner. People throw rocks, bricks, and Molotov cocktails at the agents. They shoot them. They run them down.

As Bonner noted, the escalation in violence is linked directly to enhanced enforcement efforts at the border. Forcing migration into the open desert increases the cost associated with crossing, Bonner told Congress, squeezing out small-time smugglers and increasing violent struggles to control "lucrative smuggling operations." He added that "although much of this violence is directed at rival organizations, there is an inevitable spillover that touches innocent civilians and law enforcement officials on both sides of the border."

For agents like Vasquez, the thirtyish father to a baby girl, that means taking extra care. He walks a few steps in front of me, motioning at me to stay behind him.

Caught in the Desert

We find the men we are looking for a few moments later. There are four of them, their clothes and backpacks covered in a fine layer of red dust. They put their arms up in surrender when they see Vasquez. He approaches them casually, speaking calmly.

"Do you have papers?" he asks in native Spanish. "Are you all Mexicans?"

A middle-aged man in dark green pants and a dusty blue cap singles himself out as the spokesman. "We're from Hidalgo," he says. "Illegal. I'm a farmer. So is he." He indicates one of the others with his chin. One is a carpenter, he tells us; another works in construction. "We're just here to work—we have friends in Atlanta who will give us jobs. We're not criminals."

"How long have you been walking?"

"Three days. Our coyote attacked us the first day. Shoved a revolver in his face and took everything." He jerks his head toward the youngest of the four. The young man doesn't meet my eyes. "He left us to die."

Crossing for Jobs

We'll call the man speaking Armando Ramirez. He is 49, he tells us. He says this is the first time any of them has tried to cross. None of them has ever been this far north before; none has ever seen a border town. They didn't know the way, so they paid a coyote $1,700 each. To come up with the sum, they sold everything they had. Ramirez took money from a loan shark to cover the remaining cost. "With interest," he adds. "More than 30 percent."

But there are plenty of jobs waiting for them in Atlanta, they were told. They only had to get there.

"We're here as *workers*," Ramirez says to me emphatically. "We don't smoke, we don't drink, we're not smuggling drugs— none of that. We're here to work" He glances at Vasquez. "Or *were* here to work."

Vasquez asks them to drop their bags. He checks the four men, then their packs, for weapons. He has heard all the stories before. Sometimes they're the truth, sometimes not. Coyotes often pretend to be migrants to avoid jail time and heavy fines. Smugglers sometimes hire migrants as drug mules to bring their goods into the U.S. He tends to believe these particular guys, he tells me later, but "you never know."

A Difficult Journey

"Why did you cross?" I ask them.

"I have two daughters," Ramirez says. "About your age—a 19-year-old and a 20-year-old. They want to go to school. The economic situation of our country is . . . difficult. There isn't enough money, or jobs. That's it." His eyes slide past me to the desert. A laugh—it sounds more like a bark—erupts abruptly from his throat. "One doesn't come for pleasure, that's for sure. If you can imagine how we traveled in the desert. Hardly any water. Like animals. Attacked the first day. Again the second, by a group—we didn't have anything then, at least."

His lips twist into a smile. "The coyote had taken everything, so they just beat us up. Today we found some remains in the desert. A skull, part of an arm." He shudders. "It makes one . . ."

"Scared?" Vasquez offers.

"Terrified."

"Did you have any other health problems in the journey?" Vasquez asks, noticing Ramirez's shaking hand.

Ramirez shrugs. "We're all thirsty. We ran out of water the beginning of the second day. We've been drinking out of old cattle troughs."

"That water's dirty."

"Filthy. And the flavor!" He scrunches his face in disgust, spitting for emphasis.

The End of the Journey

"If you line up, we'll go to the car and I'll get you some water."

Ramirez hesitates. He adjusts his cap and puts his hands on his hips, looking Vasquez squarely in the eye. He knows walking to the car means not only life-saving water but an end to their quest for Atlanta. "Why don't you give us a chance," he says with a jerk of his chin. "We're here to work; we're not going to hurt anyone."

Vasquez shakes his head. "I can't."

"Why not?"

"I'll lose my job."

"Why?"

"Because. It's illegal."

Ramirez looks at him for a long moment. "That's the problem, isn't it?" He stares past Vasquez into the desert. It's over 100 degrees here and has been that hot every day for the last 10 days. He's lucky to be alive. "OK, then, let's go. We understand, friend."

The four line up, Ramirez limping, and walk toward the vehicle. Vasquez and I follow closely behind.

"It's very hard to make this job look pretty," Vasquez says softly to me later, referring to Ramirez and his companions. "We're fortunate enough to live in a country where there are lots of opportunities. And most of the people who we run into out here want to make that dream happen. Unfortunately, it's our job to stop that dream. That's what we do on an everyday basis. Maybe because I'm Latino the aliens think I should understand where they're coming from. And I do, to a certain extent. But it's my job." . . .

Watching the Border

Vasquez is just one of more than 2,500 border patrol agents in the Tucson sector charged with monitoring 262 miles of border between Arizona and Sonora, and about 90,000 square miles inside the sector. Only 19 miles of the physical border is walled off (and only 2.8 miles of it in Nogales) by 14-foot-high corrugated steel landing mat left over from the Gulf War. Rusted the color of the Arizona dirt, it ambles over hills and through canyons. Ten surveillance camera towers with four cameras each—two for the day and two for the night—are scattered along the Nogales wall. Agents monitor the cameras from a control room in the Nogales Border Patrol station. If they see someone, they summon the nearest border patrol agent to the scene by radio.

Stadium-style lighting lines parts of the wall, making night look like noon. Border agents gas up and turn on portable lights every night to light the rest of the area. Seismic sensors are buried underground; triggered by footsteps, they send a signal to a radio tower that, in turn, sends a signal back to the Nogales control room.

At the edge of the town, the wall abruptly gives way to chain link fence. Then nothing. Another 31 miles of border in the Tucson sector is blocked by vehicle barriers, effective at stopping cars but not people. The rest is desert, open territory for the daring or foolhardy who want to be in America.

An Uphill Battle

The Arizona wall was built in 1999 as part of Operation Safeguard, one of a string of "deterrence" strategies implemented along the southwestern border. This strategy, which in addition to the wall building and the high-tech monitoring included assigning more agents to the border, was first employed in San Diego in 1994. By concentrating resources on key crossing areas along the Mexican frontier, mostly border towns, policy makers hoped to shut down unauthorized crossings entirely. The more remote regions—rocky mountains, desert—were expected to act as "natural" deterrents.

They didn't. As soon as the Border Patrol built the wall in San Diego, coyotes started bringing migrants to other crossing points. Rather than stopping entries, the barrier merely shifted traffic to other parts of the border. Suddenly, border residents in Texas and Arizona saw a spike of illegal crossings. Panic ensued. So authorities built more walls, shifting the traffic into the more remote desert and mountain regions. Now, the Border Patrol estimates, about 40 percent of all migrants entering the U.S. illegally in the Southwest go through Arizona—most through the desert areas where Vasquez and I met Ramirez and his friends. . . .

The Deportation Process

Armando Ramirez and his three companions wait in the back of Vasquez's truck. Soon another Border Patrol vehicle will pick them up. Ramirez will be brought to the little checkpoint along I-19 and dropped off in the trailer that acts as a de facto holding cell for migrants. Border Patrol agents will begin his paperwork before formalizing the deportation process at the Mariposa center, where they will record all 10 of his fingerprints and cross-check them with an FBI database.

If Ramirez has many prior immigration violations, he may be brought to immigration court. If he's found to be a serious criminal—a sex offender or an arsonist, say—he will be transferred to the U.S. attorney's office, where he will be held and tried. If he's found to be a first-time offender, as he claims, he will be given three options. He can have his case heard before an immigration judge. If he's afraid of returning home, he can have a hearing for amnesty. Or he can choose "voluntary return"—to be deported promptly back to his home country.

If he chooses the last option, as most do, then he'll be dropped off at the Mariposa port of entry, along with dozens of others, and escorted to Mexico with a strong admonition: Don't come back! And then he'll have to make a decision: Stay in Mexico, or try again.

They Will Be Back

"What are you going to do?" I ask.

Ramirez laughs bitterly. "What would you do?"

"I don't know."

"Do you think you will try to cross again?" Agent Vasquez wants to know.

Ramirez looks at Vasquez, then back at me. Perhaps he is thinking about the human remains he's seen. Perhaps he is thinking about the three days of walking. Of being robbed. Of his family. A deep sigh slides out. "With all due respect for the two of you," he says, "yes."

Vasquez tries to dissuade him. "It's very dangerous there. You could die. What good will you be to your family if you are dead?"

"I've thought of that."

"Look, I understand where you're coming from. But you have to understand also that it's very dangerous out there." Vasquez points out the window toward the wilderness. It's about 100 degrees today. No water. No ride. Ramirez and his friends easily could have died.

"I know." Ramirez watches as another Border Patrol vehicle pulls up beside us and slows to a stop. "But I've lost a lot of money. I just don't see any other way."

Ramirez and his friends get into the other truck. "Probably they'll try to cross again," Vasquez tells me. "They'll try their luck, see if they can make it up north to get a job."

I nod. We drive back toward Nogales to do another round of patrols.

A Minuteman Guards the Border

Charlie LeDuff

Charlie LeDuff, a staff writer for the New York Times, *contributed to the Pulitzer Prize-winning series* How Race Is Lived in America. *LeDuff is also the author of several books, including* US Guys: The True and Twisted Mind of the American Man. *In this article, LeDuff goes to the U.S. border town of Campo, California, where he spends some time with a member of the Minuteman Project. The Minutemen are private citizens who have vowed to keep illegal immigrants from crossing into the United States illegally. LeDuff gives us the story of minuteman Britt Craig, a Vietnam veteran who came home from the war wounded and felt unappreciated. After years of drifting, Craig initially came to the U.S.-Mexico border to see if a man could actually still belong to a militia. Once he got to the border, though, he saw firsthand how serious the border situation had become. Since then, he has been watching his small part of the border and patrolling areas commonly used for smuggling drugs.*

Five miles past the paved road, up on a hill of no name, lives a one-eyed man with a one-eyed cat.

They sleep in a van parked against the patchwork fence that lines the border with Mexico. He is solitary, lean, trying to hold back a tidal wave of humanity. The cat is overweight.

Britt Craig describes himself as a 57-year-old Spartan, a decorated war veteran, a Buddhist, a damaged and lonesome man, a lover of books who can pull bits of philosophy from the corners of his confinement.

"The person who has nothing for which he is willing to fight is a miserable creature and has no chance of being free unless made so and kept so by the exertions of better men than himself," Mr. Craig says in the 100-degree heat, quoting [nineteenth-century British political philosopher] John Stuart Mill almost perfectly.

He is a member of the Minuteman Project, a group of civilians dedicated to fighting illegal immigration from Mexico. He has done his part simply by standing here, watching, for 500 days.

The Minutemen claim 8,000 members, but that number is dubious at best. Consider that there are only two full-timers living on this 10-mile stretch of the 2,000-mile border now that the smuggling season is slow, the temperatures are blistering and the news media have gone on to other distractions.

A Drifter, Wounded by War

The son of a Georgia newspaperman, the grandson of a Georgia newspaperman and the great-grandson of a gentleman farmer, Mr. Craig never lived up to family expectations.

He did poorly in school and thought he would prove himself as a warrior. He enlisted as a paratrooper and lost his left eye in Vietnam. By his account, he came home to mockery and derision and this knocked him sideways.

So he drifted. Sailed. Fished. Pounded nails. Made music in Puerto Rico. Knew a few women and forgot a few women. Finally, in his later years, he grew roots on this hill. He makes his morning toilet with a bucket and a shovel.

"I never got that 1945 reception," he says from beneath the shadow of his canvas brim. "Maybe now I'm doing something the American people appreciate."

The battle disfigurement entitles him to a $2,500-a-month disability check, more than enough to cover this life in the desert.

While some, including President [George W.] Bush, call people like Mr. Craig a vigilante, more consider him a concerned citizen, if some polls are to be believed. And while the

Minutemen do carry guns, the Border Patrol says there have been no reports of immigrants being shot or abused by them since they began their campaign [in 2004].

Mr. Craig, in turn, says he has been robbed, sniped at and pelted with stones by smugglers coming across the border. There are chips in his windshield.

The Guardian of the Hill

"A society that cannot enforce its most basic rules is not a society at all," he says.

Mr. Craig, unlike some of the weekend warriors who flock to the border, is not a beer drinker from the blue-collar suburbs, a "big game hunter" or a bored retiree.

In fact, these types of Minutemen are obsequious toward this hermit on the hill. They refer to him as the Pirate, because of the patch over his ruined eye. They treat him as some sort of Colonel Kurtz [from the Vietnam War movie *Apocalypse Now*], whisper in hushed conspiratorial tones about the greatness of the warrior who sits and spends his hours thinking, watching.

"He doesn't like being approached without radio contact," says a man who goes by the moniker Gadget. "He's only got one eye, but he knows how to use it."

Out here petty jealousies, rivalries and divisions have arisen. Across the country, the Minuteman movement has splintered into a half-dozen factions, Mr. Craig answering only to himself.

There is another man who lives on a hill on the horizon to the west. He, too, is an Army veteran, a retired fisherman and a 24-hour-a-day, seven-day-a-week "scout." He flies a large American flag from a makeshift 30-foot pole, carries a .45 pistol in his waistband and lives in relative luxury in an R.V. with a port-a-potty. That man, Robert Cook, also 57, goes by the [alias] Little Dog.

Mr. Cook is annoyed that Mr. Craig will not respect his position as director of Campo border operations for the Minuteman Project. And so he has referred to Mr. Craig as a phony war hero, compared him to male genitalia and rifled off an e-mail message to CNN calling Mr. Craig a swine who lives in a cat box.

A Border Within a Border

This led to fisticuffs on the main street of town when the men happened to come off their hilltops at the same time for water and supplies. Mr. Craig, vigorous and perhaps a foot taller, gave Mr. Cook four chances to take the insults back, which Mr. Cook refused to do, ending in the breakage of Mr. Cook's eyeglasses.

The men have divided their territory at the obelisk marking the beginning of the Pacific Crest Trail, creating yet another border within the border. A reporter tried to arrange a meeting between the two.

Mr. Cook agreed. Mr. Craig refused, saying, "I'd rather see the Mexican horde pour over the border than deal with that lying runt."

"I am content to sit on a hill and sulk," he said after producing his military papers from a plastic blue pouch, which confirmed his war legacy.

An Armed Militiaman

Mr. Craig came to be a Minuteman from St. Augustine, Fla., for what he called Second Amendment reasons. Namely, he wanted to know whether a man could still belong to a militia and carry a gun on federal land. He found he could.

"But what I really found out was how messed up the border situation really is," he says. "I'm not saying we are at war. But in the course of human history, wars have always started because of one tribe pushing into the traditional boundaries of another."

And in that spirit, he has parked himself in the middle of a drug smuggling route, at serious risk to his own life. Men on horseback have uprooted his camp. Border Patrol agents testify to that. Still, Mexicans rarely cross his way anymore. They go around.

Each morning he takes his 12-gauge and his 9-millimeter pistol and inspects the smuggling paths. He lets it be known that he has respect for the young coyote [a guide paid to transport illegal immigrants across the U.S. border]. Especially the one who wears size 7 soccer cleats. Mr. Craig has often noticed his tracks.

"I respect that man immensely," he says. "I harbor no ill will against him. He's very good. I would do the same thing in his position. Still, I'd like to see those cleats hanging from my mirror like baby shoes."

Living on the Border

Leo W. Banks

Leo W. Banks is the author of numerous books, including Rattlesnake Blues: Dispatches from a Snakebit Territory. *In this piece from the* Tucson Weekly, *Banks writes about Ruth Evelyn Cowan, a rancher whose property rests near the Arizona-Mexico border. Banks writes that Cowan's property rights are routinely violated by the border-crossers that trespass on her land. Illegal immigrants routinely dump loads of trash on her land, and the human waste they leave behind has tainted her water supply. Cowan's cattle have also been adversely affected, becoming wild and unable to gain weight, causing their worth to drop in the marketplace. However, the problem has taken a larger toll on Cowan's personal life, leaving her edgy, angry, and generally causing her to feel as though the quality of her life has been altered by circumstances that are largely beyond her control.*

You couldn't find a better place to have lunch than this cramped, dusty Cochise County cook shack. It has every bit of ambience that Arizona ranch country can offer, including a wood-slat ceiling covered with strips of tin from a dismantled pigpen. In ranching, nothing goes to waste, so when Ruth Evelyn Cowan had the opportunity to collect some scrap from her parents' New Mexico ranch, she grabbed it.

The tin might rattle in the wind and drum in the rain, but those sounds create a symphony for Cowan, who loves this place and this life. She was born into it 57 years ago, and you can see that it suits her down to the mud on her boots. You don't have to listen hard to hear the contentment in her voice when she goes on about her American Brahman cattle—big, silver, hump-backed animals with floppy ears that she talks to as if they were her kids.

Leo W. Banks, "Under Siege," *Tuscon Weekly*, March 10, 2005. Reproduced by permission.

But this is Southern Arizona under siege, so there really is only one subject on the agenda, one issue that dominates all others here: the border with Mexico and the invasion of illegals who, every day and every night, rush to fill this yawning vacuum. . . .

You can't name a category of human being—good-hearted or crooked, kind or mean—or a nation, religion or ethnic group that isn't using this border to sneak into America illegally. The numbers boggle the mind. In January [2005] alone, the Border Patrol in the Tucson sector impounded 557 smuggling vehicles, confiscated 34,864 pounds of marijuana and arrested 35,704 illegals, according to agency spokesman Jose Garza.

The important number is one they can't pinpoint with certainty: how many got through. But figure it this way, using the common belief that, conservatively, for every arrest the Border Patrol makes, another two illegals make it through: With almost 500,000 arrests in the Tucson sector [in 2004], that means somewhere in the neighborhood of 1 million illegals broke into the country successfully—an average of almost 3,000 every 24 hours. And arrests for 2005 are up 10 percent, according to Garza.

Fear and Anger

Because of the sheer number of illegals—as well as their desperation, their willingness to destroy property and intimidate, and the always-simmering fear—Cowan and husband, Bob Giles, have sold most of their cattle and are significantly scaling back their ranching operation.

"I feel such relief," says Cowan of the decision she and her husband made. "I'm tired of continually looking over my shoulder. I'd like to be able to get up in the morning and not have the first part of my day spent repairing damage from the night before. I'd like to be able to live on my own ranch, but I don't feel safe there. I want a rattlesnake to be the worst thing I have to worry about. . . .

"I'm not an angry person, but I'm just ticked all the time, and that's not a healthy way to live. We're all so angry here. We're tired of the apathy of people who live elsewhere. What's happening here is everyone's problem, not just ours. We're tired of people who live in another country thumbing their noses at our laws, our culture and our customs, and threatening what we've spent generations building. . . .

"I'm a rich rancher," Cowan says, her tone mocking the very idea. "Well, I guess I *am* rich in a way. I have my husband, my parents, my friends, the ability to work and make a living. As far as cash in my pocket, I don't have that. Financially, I've been devastated. But I feel spiritually, emotionally and physically bankrupt, too. In my lifetime, I've never been where I am today. I don't want to see the damage the illegals have done anymore, I don't want to look at it; I don't want to fix it. That's a whole new me, because I'm 9-foot-tall and bulletproof. The illegals have changed everything."

Caught in the Path of Smugglers

She's right, and it's happening up and down the Arizona-Mexico border. A way of life is being run through a grinder. The way people think, how they go about their days, the way they work, the way they view the government—everything is changing. The smuggling trade has done this, by its sheer vastness, by the corrupting profits it produces.

Four Mexican towns abutting the Arizona border—Cananea, Altar, Naco and Agua Prieta—once quiet, traditional, mostly safe, anchored by a few old families, have become the primary smuggler-staging grounds. Their central plazas bustle with men, women and children who stay in the hotels, eat at the restaurants, buy hats, water bottles, clothes and shoes, and lounge around in public until it's time to hop a cab up to the line.

With them comes a post office wall full of bad guys allied with the movement of people and drugs north—enforcers, cutthroat coyotes, gang bosses, gang soldiers and on and on. Ordinary Mexicans, those not involved in the trade, don't like seeing these people filling their streets, the smugglers or their charges. They view the latter just as many Southern Arizonans do—as invaders.

They're from somewhere else. They dress differently. They look different. Fearful parents in these towns order their kids to stay indoors because they don't want them playing near the strangers. They call them *crosseros*, Spanish for "crossers." Stay away from the crossers, they tell their kids.

Losing Faith in Government

Close to dark, the cabs move out. From the right hilltop vantage point on the Arizona side, you can set up a lawn chair, fire up a cheap cigar and watch the invasion. You see the headlights streaming north, virtual convoys of Ford Crown Vics and beat-up old Mercurys filled to the windows with soon-to-be illegals. From Cananea—where a legal taxi permit now costs an astonishing $15,000—they follow a dirt road that splits about 10 miles south of the border, one fork leading to the San Rafael Valley, in the mountains above Patagonia; the other to the San Pedro River Valley. In some cases, their feet don't hit the ground until they're literally a quarter-mile from the international fence.

It's an enormous business, and by any measure, a historic migration that is profoundly changing our country. But none of it is happening according to anybody's plan, certainly no American legislative body, and here's the biggest rub—it's a revolution of appetites. Mexico benefits by dumping off its poorest, avoiding the thorny responsibility of taking care of its own people, and it benefits from the cash these laborers send home, which, after oil, now constitutes that government's second-largest income source. But American appetites contribute greatly as well, specifically, our appetite for cheap labor and illicit drugs, which creates this powerful magnet effect, pulling people and dope to the border.

For those living on the line, that might be the worst of it—the recognition that their own people help fuel the daily chaos in which they live. It breeds in good citizens a corrosive cynicism, especially toward government—the same government to which they've been loyal all their lives, and to which they pay taxes and rely on for protection. . . .

Life in a War Zone

We're in Cowan's pickup truck now, driving across a broad stretch of southeast Arizona on an inspection tour of the war zone. The road we're traveling, Davis Road, is a particular menace, a stretch of hot blacktop that connects Highway 80, near Tombstone, with Highway 191 above Douglas.

It doesn't look especially perilous as it rolls over its 23-mile course. But the frequent dips and doglegs can leave drivers blind and at the mercy of smugglers who screech around the turns, sometimes at 100 mph. Cowan has twice been run off this road, and like others in the vicinity, she avoids traveling here at night. But she can't avoid it entirely, because portions of her 17,000-acre spread straddle Davis Road. . . .

Cowan keeps her own gun stashed under the console of her truck as we drive Davis Road, a supremely sane thing to do in a place where automatic-weapons fire from drug runners shatters the night quiet, and the daytime signs of smuggling are everywhere. Just look around: hubcaps hooked to range fences—signals for coyotes or druggies to cross there; cars with Florida and California plates, probably stolen, wheeling up and down the road; cattle gates mangled by smuggler cars. Cowan says every single gate along Davis Road has been smashed at least once.

With her weekend's work as a flight attendant done, Cowan would return to Arizona to run the ranch. Her husband, Bob, now 58, who lives and works in Phoenix running his own company, would drive the 200 miles to Tombstone, work with her on Saturdays and Sundays, then drive the 200 miles back to Phoenix on Sunday night. "It was very hard," Bob Giles says. "I wonder now how the hell I survived it. But we needed the money I sent down there to run the ranch."

But the damage caused by illegals in Cowan's absence kept getting worse, which made going to work a peculiar torture. She knew the odds were good that something bad was happening back on the ranch, but she didn't know what it was, and couldn't do anything about it anyway. "If I'm in Japan, what can I do about a problem in Arizona?" she asks. "All I can do is worry. It got to the point where I stopped calling home."

Illegal immigration became the hell that followed her around the world. There was no escaping it.

The Effects on Personal Property

On work weekends, her routine was to drive to Phoenix, catch a flight to L.A. and begin whatever assignment she had from Northwest. But while parking at the Phoenix airport, she said, she'd sometimes spot vehicles that she'd seen crossing her property the day before. The van or truck would park, and a dozen or more illegals would jump out, then head to the terminals to catch flights all across the country.

Sometimes, Cowan says, they were even on her flight to L.A., and because she speaks fluent Spanish, she was often asked to translate for, quite possibly, the very same individuals who'd just trashed her property.

"So many things have happened; I can't remember the chronology," Cowan says as we drive. "It all blends together."

She points to a pasture out the driver's window. "See, over there, I have a water line they keep cutting. So I rigged a faucet to it so they could drink without letting thousands of gallons drain out. But now they don't turn off the faucet, so the water runs out anyway."

Three north-south smuggling trails cross Cowan's land, and so many illegals walk them that they spooked her cattle, making them wild. Wild cattle don't gain as much weight, and when ranchers go to market, they sell quality and weight. She also followed a specific breeding program, but with her gates constantly left open and fences cut, her herds were becoming mongrelized and more susceptible to disease from neighboring cattle.

The Waste They Leave Behind

Cowan takes pride in how she manages her property, and in the past six years, she's received more than $375,000 in various grants for watershed rehabilitation. But the illegals leave behind piles and piles of human feces, which, after a rain, drain into the gullies and into the water supply.

"Should we test to see whether the feces in the water is from cows or people?" she asks. "In some places on my land, the native grasses have been trampled so heavily they won't grow back in my lifetime, and I'll be blamed."

In October [2004], she had nine at-risk kids out on the ranch picking up the illegals' garbage. They bagged a spectacular 6,080 pounds over five days. Four months later, it was all back again. She once called the EPA [Environmental Protection Agency] to report dumping of trash on state trust land. "Who's doing the dumping?" the bureaucrat asked.

"Illegals."

"Oh," said the bureaucrat. "We don't have a department to deal with that." . . .

A Chilling Warning

One day, Cowan came across a blue Chevy pickup with a camper shell parked off Davis Road. Opposite it, on the other side of the road, there was a man standing near his truck. He pretended to be inspecting a sign that Cowan had put up. It said: "If this were Crawford, Texas, the National Guard would be here." She knew immediately the man was spotting for a coyote. She drove up to him and rolled down the window. He was Anglo, middle-aged, with tattoos along both arms and bright blue eyes.

In a sickeningly sweet voice, he said, "Oh, do you have a problem with illegals around here?"

Right then, the Chevy across the street bolted toward Tombstone. Even though she was pulling a 16-foot stock trailer, Cowan roared off in pursuit, punching 911 on her cell as she went. Tombstone's marshals intercepted the Chevy, finding 19 illegals inside. It was a good outcome, except that the coyotes, listening in on police scanners, heard everything the dispatcher and the deputies said. A few days later, a relative with ties to the sheriff's office delivered a chilling warning to Cowan: The coyotes know who you are, and they know where you are, so watch your back.

No Escaping the Invasion

Night begins to fall over a long day in the war zone. We're on Leslie Canyon Road, north of Douglas. It's two lanes, no traffic, mostly pastureland straddling the blacktop. One of the pastures belongs to Cowan, and there's a red truck parked on the shoulder near her pasture gate, two men standing beside it. They have no reason for being there, and they're acting strange.

Cowan drives a mile past the gate, pulls to the shoulder to wait, and we talk some more. She has remained even-tempered through the day, in the telling of every wrenching episode, and she has tried to keep perspective. She acknowledges that many factors have contributed to the difficulties of ranching in Southern Arizona—everything from the nine-year drought to housing development that has brought dogs that run in packs, killing calves.

But the illegals have been the tipping point. She could survive everything else. She can't survive the invasion. "It just consumes you," she says. "If you're not at a meeting talking about it, you're repairing something they've done, or you're standing on the highway looking at a dead animal, because they left a gate open. You have to decide: Is this more important than my quality of life, my health, my marriage?" . . .

The Emotional Toll

We double back—to check on the mysterious red truck and the two men. They're gone. Then Cowan spots them again, down the pasture road, about a half-mile beyond the gate. The men have cut the lock, closed the gate again and looped the chain back into place. You have to look closely to see it, which is no doubt what they wanted.

Now it starts—the uncertainty, the jangled nerves. Who are these guys? Are they using the pasture for a drug drop? Are these the coyotes out to get even with Cowan?

She gets on her cell and calls the Cochise County sheriff. Then we wait, wondering if this time, she'll have to pull that gun.

It's a rotten feeling. It shouldn't be this way. For the first time all day, Cowan's temper cracks, and under the strain, she cries. She makes a fist. "I feel so violated. I just get wound up so tight I want to scream. It's just goes on and on and on, every day."

This event ends much better than it might have. The men tell sheriff's deputies they're Douglas residents and American citizens out hunting for the afternoon. They claim the lock was already cut when they came along. Cowan wants to press charges, saying she's placed legal notices in three area newspapers, describing the property in English and Spanish and stating that her land is off limits to hunters, and the pasture fence is plastered with "Keep Out" signs.

But on the border, gates mean nothing. Your possessions are up for grabs. Private property means nothing.

Organizations to Contact

The editors have compiled the following list of organizations concerned with the issues debated in this book. The descriptions are derived from materials provided by the organizations. All have publications or information available for interested readers. The list was compiled on the date of publication of the present volume; the information provided here may change. Be aware that many organizations take several weeks or longer to respond to inquiries, so allow as much time as possible.

American Civil Liberties Union (ACLU)
125 Broad St., 18th Fl., New York, NY   10004
(212) 567-ACLU (membership; other numbers vary by state)
e-mail: aclucorrespond@aclu.org
Web site: www.aclu.org

The American Civil Liberties Union is a nonprofit, nonpartisan group working to protect First Amendment rights, the right to privacy, due process laws, and equal protection under the law. Annually, its members handle nearly six thousand court cases from every state in the union in defense of these rights. The ACLU is a leading advocate for the rights of immigrants, refugees, and noncitizens, challenging unconstitutional laws and practices and countering what it sees as the myths upon which many of these laws are based.

American Immigration Control Foundation
222 W. Main St., Monterey, VA   24465
(540) 468-2022 • fax: (540) 468-2024
e-mail: aicfndn@ntelos.net
Web site: www.aicfoundation.com

The American Immigration Control Foundation, founded in 1983, is one of the nation's oldest immigration reform organizations. Representing many different ethnic groups and backgrounds, the foundation is committed to preserving

Americans' common heritage and to helping educate U.S. citizens on the harmful effects of uncontrolled immigration. To raise public awareness, the foundation has produced and distributed numerous books, monographs, pamphlets, and videos, which are available on its Web site.

American Immigration Law Foundation (AILF)
918 F St. NW, 6th Fl., Washington, DC   20004
(202) 742-5600 • fax: (202) 742-5619
e-mail: info@ailf.org
Web site: www.ailf.org

The American Immigration Law Foundation is a nonprofit organization dedicated to increasing public understanding of immigration law and policy and the value of immigration to U.S. society. It advances fundamental fairness and due process under the law for immigrants. Through the Legal Action Center, Immigration Policy Center, and Public Education Program, AILF members advocate and litigate on behalf of immigrants, author policy papers on the beneficial effects of immigration for the United States, and educate youth on the United States as historically a "nation of immigrants."

Americans for Immigration Control (AIC)
PO Box 738, Monterey, VA   24465
(540) 468-2023 • fax: (540) 468-2026
e-mail: aic@immigrationcontrol.com
Web site: www.immigrationcontrol.com

Americans for Immigration Control is the largest grassroots lobby for immigration reform. Its missions are to increase funding and manpower of the U.S. Border Patrol, assign U.S. military troops to help the Border Patrol regain control of the southern border, reduce legal immigration levels, end most federal public assistance to noncitizens, and to repeal federal bilingual education programs and bilingual balloting. It works to accomplish these goals through petitions and letter-writing campaigns to legislators and numerous television and media appearances.

Border Angels
PO Box 86598, San Diego, CA   92138
(619) 269-7865
e-mail: enriquemorones@cox.net
Web site: www.borderangels.org

Founded by Enrique Morones in 1986, Border Angels is a nonprofit organization staffed by volunteers who provide water and clothing as well as other aid to illegal immigrants crossing the border. The group works to prevent the high number of deaths resulting from extreme weather conditions as well as some racial-discrimination crimes. Educating citizens and government officials on the status of weather-related deaths and racial-discrimination-crime deaths is a major goal of Border Angels.

Cato Institute
1000 Massachusetts Ave. NW, Washington, DC   20001-5403
(202) 842-0200 • fax: (202) 842-3490
e-mail: dgriswold@cato.org
Web site: www.cato.org

The Cato Institute is a nonprofit libertarian public policy research organization advocating limited government, individual liberty, free markets, and peace. The institute maintains an extensive publishing program dealing with a spectrum of public policy issues. Books, monographs, briefing papers, and shorter studies are commissioned on various aspects of the public policy debate, including immigration. Cato's research program on labor markets and immigration highlights how open, competitive, and flexible labor markets lead to a more dynamic economy and higher living standards. Its scholars often argue that immigrants are a net benefit to the U.S. economy.

Center for American Progress
1333 H St. NW, 10th Fl., Washington, DC   20005
(202) 682-1611
e-mail: progress@americanprogress.org
Web site: www.americanprogress.org

The Center for American Progress is a progressive think tank dedicated to improving the lives of Americans through ideas and action. The organization asserts that the United States should be a country of boundless opportunity in which all people can improve themselves through education, hard work, and the freedom to pursue their aspirations. The group works for an open and effective government that champions the common good over narrow self-interest, harnesses the strength of U.S. diversity, and secures the rights and safety of its people. The center favors immigration reform that includes amnesty for illegal immigrants and federal programs that facilitate immigrant assimilation.

Center for Immigration Studies (CIS)
1522 K St. NW, Suite 820, Washington, DC   20005-1202
(202) 466-8185 • fax: (202) 466-8076
e-mail: center@cis.org
Web site: www.cis.org

The Center for Immigration Studies is an independent, non-partisan research organization. It is the nation's only think tank devoted exclusively to research and policy analysis of the economic, social, demographic, fiscal, and other impacts of immigration on the United States. The center's mission is to expand public knowledge and understanding of the need for an immigration policy that gives first concern to the broad national interest. The CIS is motivated by a pro-immigrant, low-immigration vision that seeks fewer immigrants but a warmer welcome for those admitted.

Federation for American Immigration Reform (FAIR)
1666 Connecticut Ave. NW, Suite 400
Washington, DC   20009
(202) 328-7004 • fax: (202) 387-3447
e-mail: bdane@fairus.org
Web site: www.fairus.org

The Federation for American Immigration Reform is a national, public-interest membership organization of concerned citizens who share a common belief that U.S. immigration policies must be reformed to serve the national interest. FAIR seeks to improve border security, to stop illegal immigration, and to promote immigration levels consistent with its understanding of the national interest. FAIR's publications and research are used by academics and government officials in preparing new legislation, and its members have been called on to testify on congressional immigration bills more than any organization in the United States.

Minuteman Project
c/o Jim Gilchrist, Laguna Hills, CA 92654
(949) 587-5199 • fax: (949) 222-6607
e-mail: century21minuteman@sbcglobal.net
Web site: www.minutemanproject.com

Jim Gilchrist founded the Minuteman Project in 2004, after years of unsuccessful efforts trying to get the U.S. government to enforce existing immigration laws. Gilchrist describes himself as a passionate defender of the First Amendment of the U.S. Constitution and an avid supporter of law enforcement organizations. Gilchrist believes that many people want the United States to be governed by the rule of law. He urges proactive enforcement of U.S. national security protections and the immigration legal code.

Pew Hispanic Center
1615 L St. NW, Suite 700, Washington, DC 20036-5610
(202) 419-3600 (main) • fax: (202) 419-3608
e-mail: info@pewhispanic.org
Web site: www.pewhispanic.org

The Pew Hispanic Center's mission is to improve understanding of the U.S. Hispanic population and to chronicle Latinos' growing impact on the United States. The center does not advocate for nor take positions on policy issues. Instead, it conducts and commissions scholarly studies on a wide range of topics that are written to be accessible to the general public. The center also regularly conducts public opinion surveys that intend to disseminate Latino views on a range of social matters and public policy issues, including immigration, labor, demography, and economics.

ProEnglish
1601 N. Kent St., Suite 1100, Arlington, VA   22209
(703) 816-8821 • fax: (703) 816-8824
e-mail: mail@proenglish.org
Web site: www.proenglish.org

ProEnglish is a member-supported, national nonprofit organization working to make English the official language of the United States. Since its creation in 1994, ProEnglish has been an advocate for English-only education and for ending tax-funded bilingual programs and translation services. In addition to doing research and conducting a wide variety of public education activities to advance its goal, ProEnglish has specialized in providing pro-bono legal assistance to public and private agencies facing litigation or regulatory actions over language.

United States Citizenship and Immigration Services (USCIS)
(800) 375-5283
e-mail: uscis.webmaster@dhs.gov
Web site: www.uscis.gov

The USCIS, a part of the Department of Homeland Security, administers immigration and naturalization adjudication functions and establishes immigration services policies and priorities. These functions include adjudication of immigrant visa petitions, naturalization petitions, and asylum and refugee applications. The agency comprises fifteen thousand federal employees and contractors working in approximately 250 field offices around the world.

Bibliography

Books

Richard Alba and Victor Nee	*Remaking the American Mainstream: Assimilation and Contemporary Immigration.* Cambridge, MA: Harvard University Press, 2005.
Larry Blasko	*Opening the Borders.* Jamul, CA: Level 4, 2007.
Justin Akers Chacon and Mike Davis	*No One Is Illegal: Fighting Violence and State Repression on the U.S.- Mexico Border.* Chicago: Haymarket, 2006.
Aviva Chomsky	*"They Take Our Jobs!": and 20 Other Myths About Immigration.* Boston: Beacon, 2007.
Roger Daniels	*Guarding the Golden Door: American Immigration Policy and Immigrants Since 1882.* New York: Hill and Wang, 2004.
Jorge Durand, Nolan J. Malone, and Douglas S. Massey	*Beyond Smoke and Mirrors: Mexican Immigration in an Era of Economic Integration.* New York: Russell Sage Foundation, 2003.
Otis L. Graham Jr.	*Unguarded Gates: A History of America's Immigration Crisis.* Lanham, MD: Rowman & Littlefield, 2006.

J.D. Hayworth   *Whatever It Takes: Illegal Immigration, Border Security and the War on Terror*. Washington, DC: Regnery, 2007.

Peter Kivisto   Incorporating Diversity: Rethinking Assimilation in a Multicultural Age. Boulder, CO: Paradigm, 2005.

Sonia Nazario   *Enrique's Journey*. New York: Random House, 2006.

Mae M. Ngai   *Impossible Subjects: Illegal Aliens and the Making of Modern America*. Princeton, NJ: Princeton University Press, 2004.

Alejandro Portes and Rubén G. Rumbaut   *Immigrant America: A Portrait*. Berkeley and Los Angeles: University of California Press, 2006.

Erik Rush   *Solving the Border Problem Through Annexation and Assimilation*. Jamul, CA: Level 4, 2007.

Peter A. Schulkin   *A Layman's Guide to the Illegal Immigration Problem*. Charleston, SC: Booksurge, 2007.

Daniel Sheehy   *Fighting Immigration Anarchy*. Bloomington, IN: Rooftop, 2006.

Carol M. Swain   *Debating Immigration*. New York: Cambridge University Press, 2007.

Tom Tancredo   *In Mortal Danger: The Battle for America's Border and Security*. Nashville, TN: Cumberland House, 2006.

Daniel J. Tichenor *Dividing Lines: The Politics of Immigration Control in America.* Princeton, NJ: Princeton University Press, 2002.

Luis Alberto Urrea *The Devil's Highway: A True Story.* New York: Little, Brown, 2004.

Michele Wucker *Lockout: Why America Keeps Getting Immigration Wrong When Our Prosperity Depends on Getting It Right.* New York: PublicAffairs, 2006.

Periodicals

Perry Bacon Jr. "Wrestling with Immigration," *Time,* May 6, 2006.

Holly Bailey, Evan Thomas, and Richard Wolffe "Bush's Spanish Lessons," *Newsweek,* May 29, 2006.

Cecilia Balli "The Border Is Wide: Guarding the Southern Flank of the American Dream," *Harper's,* October 2006.

Stephen Barr "One Tired, Undertrained, Overworked Face at the Border," *Washington Post,* November 14, 2007.

Jeffrey Bell "The Coming Immigration Deal," *Weekly Standard,* June 19, 2006.

Arian Campo-Flores "A Xenophobic Zeitgeist," *Newsweek,* September 24, 2007.

Gregory Clark "Aid That Jumps the Border," *Los Angeles Times,* July 31, 2007.

Economist	"Death in the Desert," August 25, 2007.
Economist	"The Rusty Grenade," November 18, 2006.
Thomas B. Edsall	"Border Politics," *National Journal*, February 10, 2007.
Mary Engel	"Study Finds Immigrants' Use of Healthcare System Lower than Expected," *Los Angeles Times*, November 27, 2007.
Samuel G. Freedman	"Church Expands Mission to Immigration Advocacy," *New York Times*, September 8, 2007.
Sarah Garland	"Immigrant Nation," *Marie Claire*, September 2006.
David Gonzalez	"Raising Young Voices," *New York Times*, July 16, 2007.
Eamon Javers	"The Divided States of America," *Business Week*, April 16, 2007.
Miriam Jordan	"Anti-Immigration Activists Roil the Heartland," *Wall Street Journal*, July 16, 2007.
Angie C. Marek	"Border Battles," *U.S. News & World Report*, June 25, 2007.
Emma Marris	"Wildlife Caught in Crossfire of U.S. Immigration Battle," *Nature*, July 27, 2006.

Janet Novack   "Who's Gonna Do the Work?" *Forbes*,
                      October 1, 2007.

Andrea Batiste   "Pro-Immigrant Populism," *Nation*,
Schlesinger   March 5, 2007.

Nathan   "The Case for Amnesty," *Time*, June
Thornburgh   7, 2007.

Time   "Illegal in America," June 18, 2007.

Jesse Walker   "Exploitation or Expulsion," *Reason*,
                      August 2006.

Bryan Welch   "Putting a Stop to Slave Labor," *Utne*,
                      March/April 2007.

Index

A

ACLU (American Civil Liberties Union), 15
AFL-CIO (American Federation of Labor and Congress of Industrial Organizations), 146
African Americans, 36–37
African Resources Center, 32
Agricultural Jobs (AgJOBS) bill, 132
Alivio Medical Center, 101
American agriculture, 62–63
American Civil Liberties Union (ACLU), 15
American Enterprise Institute, 41
American Federation of Labor and Congress of Industrial Organizations (AFL-CIO), 146
The American Prospect (magazine), 46
Amnesty, 122–123
    immigration politics, 141–142
    legalization and, 146–147
    Z visa, 135–137, 139
Amstutz, Steve, 90
Arizona, 138, 152–153
    alternative spending scenarios, 82
    Chamber of Commerce and Industry, 153
    Children's Health Insurance Program, 97
    Copper Queen Community Hospital, 98
    Maricopa Medical, 98
    Southeast Arizona Medical Center, 98
    Tucson University Medical Center, 98

Assimilation, 30
    assessment, 29
    economic, 36
    intermarriage, 38–39
    multigenerational, 29, 34
    patterns, 32–33
    social, 38–39
Australia, 67–68

B

Baltimore Sun (newspaper), 56
Barone, Michael, 45
Bonner, T.J., 171
Border crossing, 155–157, 160, 184
Border Integrity and Immigration Reform Act, 118–119, 122
Border patrol agents, 19, 168–171, 174
Border security, 96, 118–121
Boston Route 128, 68
Brownsville Medical Center, 100
Buena Vista County hospital, 101
Bush Administration (George W.), 28, 44
Bush, George W., 23, 41, 69, 118, 128

C

California
    alternative spending scenarios, 79–80
    El Centro Regional Medical Center, 99
    emergency rooms, 99
    fiscal politics, 46
    hospitals, 98–99
    immigrant costs, 65
    Latinoization, 46

Orange County Community Clinic, 99

Pioneers Memorial Hospital, 99

Scripps Memorial Hospital, 99

uninsured farm workers, 109

University of California Medical Center at Irvine, 103

Campaign for Fiscal Equity, 80

Cato Institute, 69

CBO (Congressional Budget Office), 70, 83

Center for American Common Culture, 31

Center for American Progress, 105

Center for Immigration Studies, 30, 43

Center for Trade Policy Studies, 69

Center on Budget and Policy Priorities, 81

Chacon, Justin, 141

Chavez, Cesar, 144

Chicago, 35–36, 101

Children, 22, 29, 108

Children's Health Insurance Program, Arizona, 97

Children's Hospital & Regional Medical Center, Seattle, 104

Children's Memorial Hospital, Chicago, 101

Christian Science Monitor (newspaper), 159

Citizen and Immigration Services, Department of Homeland Security, 28

City Journal (magazine), 53, 58

City surveys, 25–26

Class warfare, 46–47

Clueless (film), 44

Colorado, 82–83

Colorado Horse Park, 122

Committee on Homeland Security and Governmental Affairs, 14

Comprehensive Immigration Reform Act (2006), 14, 70, 133

Congressional Budget Office (CBO), 70, 83–84

Congressional Research Service, 83–84

Construction workers, 63–64

Copper Queen Community Hospital, Arizona, 98

Cornyn, John, 99

Coyotes, 155–156, 171–173

Crime, 21, 170
    data, 48–50
    inmate population, 73
    sex crimes, 50–51
    U.S. rate, 73
    violent, 73

Cultural integration, 14, 30–31

Customs and Border Protection, 118

D

Daily News-Record (newspaper), 48

Day laborers, 64, 112–113

Deficit Reduction Act (2005), 106, 109

Department of Homeland Security, 28, 135

Deportation, 52–54, 128–129, 175–176

Drunk-driving, 55–56

E

Economic studies, 70–71

Education
    funds division, 90
    in-state tuition discounts, 83–84
    Mexican Americans, 37–39, 42–43, 60, 67
    migrant families, 161–167

public school overcrowding, 72–73

state funding, 77–78

undocumented students, 86–90

Education Funding Reform Act (2005), 80

El Centro Pioneers Memorial Hospital, 99

El Centro Regional Medical Center, 99

El Paso Thomason General Hospital, 100

Employers, 19, 123

health care costs, 92

sanctions, enforcement, 22, 24, 125, 152–153

temporary worker program, 123–125

Employment, 21–22

day laborers, 64, 112–113

health insurance, 95

low-skilled workers, 60–61

Mexican *vs.* African Americans, 36–37

modernization and, 62–63

native workers, 61–62

U.S., 59–60

wages, 43, 61–63

See also Guest-worker programs

English-only legislation, 12–15

Essential Worker Immigration Coalition, 144

Ethnic enclaves, 32, 35, 67

F

Federation for American Immigration Reform (FAIR), 77, 92

Fix, Michael, 29

Flake-Kolbe-McCain immigration bill, 69

Florida

alternative spending scenarios, 81

Broward County, 100

Florida Hospital Association, 100–101

hospitals, 100–101

uninsured non-U.S. citizens, 100

Florida Hospital Association, 100–101

Fonte, John, 31

Free Trade Bulletin (magazine), 69

Friedman, Milton, 60

Frist, Bill, 142

G

GAO (Government Accounting Office), 49–50, 137

Georgia, 81–82

Giuliani, Rudolph, 55

Gonzalez, Emilio, 28

Government

role, services, 22, 28, 94

spending, 31, 70, 94

training conferences, 28

websites, 28

Government Accounting Office (GAO), 49–50, 137

Grandview School District, 162–164, 166–167

Great Society program, 164

Green card reforms, 130

Guest-worker programs, 111–112, 130

organized labor and, 144–145

politics, 142–143

public health system, 111–112

rights, 144

H

Harris County Hospital District, 100
Harvest of Shame (film), 162
Hastert, Dennis, 143
Heritage Foundation, 69
HISD (Houston Independent School District), 85–91
Hispanic students, HISD, 91
Home Depot, 64
H1-B visas, 68
Hospital burden, 73–74, 96–97
    Arizona, 97–98
    California, 98–99
    Chicago, 101
    Florida, 100–101
    Minnesota, 102
    New Jersey, 101
    New York, 102
    North Carolina, 102
    Pennsylvania, 101
    service curtailment, 103
    South Carolina, 101
    Texas, 99–100
    travel costs, 102
Houston Chronicle (newspaper), 85
Houston Independent School District (HISD), 85–91
How Race Is Lived in America (series), 178
H2-A visas, 111–112
Hudson Institute, 31

I

ICE (Immigration and Customs Enforcement), 135–136
Illegal immigration
    children, 22, 29, 108
    crime data, 48–50
    drunk-driving, 55–56
    estimates, 119

Illegal Immigration Reform and Immigrant Responsibility Act of 1996 (IIRAIRA), 92
Illinois, 80
Immigrants
    adult *vs.* children, 29
    construction workers, 63–64
    economic costs, 60, 65–66, 70–72
    family, 157–158
    health rates, 113
    health services use, 73–74, 110–111
    income, tax compliance, 65, 115
    intergenerational success, 36–37
    job skills, 130
    legal status, 21–22, 132, 146–147
Immigration
    conservative advocates, 46
    enforcement, 92
    European *vs.* Mexican, 35–36, 39
    history, 34
    legal *vs.* illegal, 21–22
    motivation, 157–158
    numbers, 59
    percentage, 29
    political Left and, 45
    politics, 141–142
    positive perceptions, 20–21
    reducing, 84
    reform, 69–70, 128, 130–131
    restricting, 71, 112
    roads and, 72
    sex crimes, 50–53
    social program use, 65–66
    uninsured, 94–95, 100, 107–109
Immigration and Customs Enforcement (ICE), 135–136

Immigration and Naturalization Service (INS), 53

Immigration Policy Center (IPC), 73

Inhofe, James, 14

INS (Immigration and Naturalization Service), 53

In-state tuition discounts, 83–84

Instructional resources, 14–15

Intermarriage, 38–39

IPC (Immigration Policy Center), 73

Italians Then, Mexicans Now (Perlmann), 39

J

Jamaica Hospital, 102

Johnson, Lyndon, 164

Just So No To Amnesty campaign, 142

K

Kamus, Abdul, 32

Kauflin, Deborah, 50–51

Kenan Institute of Private Enterprise, 75

Kennedy, Ted, 133, 142

King, Steve, 142

Krieble, Helen, 121–122

Krikorian, Mark, 30

Kyl, Jon, 152

L

Language gap, 12

Las Vegas, 25

Lee High School, 85, 90

Legislative initiatives, 12, 92–93, 148–153

Los Angeles, 53–54

Los Angeles Times (newspaper), 53, 143

Louisiana Purchase, 16

Low-skilled workers, 60–61

M

Manhattan Institute, 42, 53, 58

Maricopa Medical, Arizona, 98

McCain, John, 128, 142

McDonald, Heather, 53–55

Medicaid, 94, 103–104, 106

Merry Maids, 44

Mexican Americans
    education, 37–39, 42–43, 60, 67
    emerging subclass, 43–44
    employment, 36–37
    intermarriage, 38–39
    wage gap, 43

Mexico
    rapto concept, 52
    U.S. border, 96, 118–121, 149, 155, 168–169

Meyerson, Harold, 46

Migrant Education Program, 164–166

Migrant families, workers, 13, 63, 161–167

Migrant Legal Action Program, 161

Migrant Policy Institute, 145

Migrant Student Information Exchange, 165

Migrant Student Records Transfer System, 165

Migration Policy Institute, 30–31

Minnesota, 102

Minutemen Project, 179–182

Mujica, Mauro, 13–14

N

Napolitano, Janet, 152
National Academy of Sciences (NAS), 64–65
National Advisory Committee on Rural Health, 97
National Agricultural Workers Survey, 162
National Assessment of Education Progress, 81
National Association of Counties, 93, 95
National Association of State Directors of Migrant Education, 165
National Center on Immigrant Integration Policy, 30
National Conference of State Legislatures (NCSL), 150
National ID card, 22, 139
National Immigration Law Center, 149
National Public Radio, 148
National Research Council (NRC), 70–71, 74, 115
National Review (magazine), 41
Native Americans, 16
NCLB (No Child Left Behind Act), 164–165
NCSL (National Conference of State Legislatures), 150
Negative Population Growth, 92
New American (magazine), 48, 52
The New Americans: Economic, Demographic, and Fiscal Effects of Immigration (study), 71
New Deal, 46
New Jersey, 80–81, 101
New York, 55, 64
    alternative spending scenarios, 80

hospitals, 102
Jamaica Hospital, 102
New York Times (newspaper), 14, 178
Newcomer's Charter School, 85–86, 90
No Child Left Behind Act (NCLB), 164–165
No One Is Illegal: Fighting Violence and State Repression on the U.S.-Mexico border (Chacon), 141
North Carolina, 25, 82, 102
NRC (National Research Council), 70–71

O

Operation Return to Sender, 49–51, 53
Operation Safeguard, 175
Orange County Community Clinic, 99
Orellana, Alcides, 33
Our Country (Barone), 45

P

Pederson, Jim, 152
Pennsylvania, 101
Perlmann, Joel, 39–40
Personal Responsibility and Work Opportunity Reconciliation Act (1996), 71, 94, 106–107
Pew Hispanic Center, 20, 118
Pew Research Center, 18, 20
Phoenix, Arizona, 20, 25
Pioneers Memorial Hospital, 99
Plyler v. Doe, 85–86, 90
Policy solutions, 75–76
Political leadership, 23–24, 55
Politicians, 12, 127, 141–142
Poverty, 95
Private property, 188–192

Public Agenda survey, 41–42
Public health system
    cost shifting, 113
    day workers, 112–113
    employers and, 92
    free riders, 114–115
    guest-worker programs, 111–112
    health care premiums, 116
    hospitals, 73–74, 92, 96–104
    immigrants use, 105–106, 110–111, 115–116
    misconceptions, 106
    public cost, 95–96
    state and local governments, 92, 103–104, 108, 114–115
    uninsured, 94–95, 100, 107–109
Public opinion, 18–22
    ideological, 23–25
    proximity factor, 22–23
    socioeconomic, 24
Public schools, 72–73, 85–91
    See also Education

R

Rand Corporation, 74
Rape cases, 51–53
Reagan, Ronald, 44
Regional Medical Center, El Centro, 99
Reid, T.R., 148
Resendiz, Angel, 52–53
Roads, 72
Roosevelt, Franklin Delano, 46
Roosevelt, Theodore, 15
Rove, Karl, 46
Ruiz, Hernan, 27–28

S

Sacramento Bee (newspaper), 144
Sanctuary cities, 53–54, 135–136

SCHIP (State Children's Health Insurance Program), 106–108
Scripps Memorial Hospital, 99
Seattle Children's Hospital & Regional Medical Center, 104
Senate Judiciary Committee on Immigration Policy, 127
Service Employees Industrial Union (SEIU), 145
Sex crimes, 50–51
S.I. Hayawaka Official English Language Bill, 14
Silicon Valley, 68
Social Security Administration (SSA), 115
South Carolina, 101
Southeast Arizona Medical Center, 98
Specter, Arlen, 128, 143
State and local governments, 12, 77–78
    alternative spending scenarios, 79–83
    criminal legislation, 151–152
    federal government and, 150–151
    in-state tuition discounts, 83–84
    low-skilled immigrants and, 74–75
    Medicaid restrictions, 103
    multistate approach, 149–150
    public health care funding, 92, 103–104, 108, 114–115
State Children's Health Insurance Program (SCHIP), 99, 106–108
Strengthening America's Communities, 81

T

Tancredo, Tom, 142
Task Force on New Americans, 28

Temporary worker program, 24, 46, 123, 130–132

Terrorism, terrorists, 21, 118, 134–140

Texas
alternative spending scenarios, 80
Brownsville Medical Center, 100
El Paso Thomason General Hospital, 100
Harris County Hospital District, 100
hospitals, 99–100
Plyler v. Doe, 85–86, 90
State Children's Health Insurance Program, 99
undocumented students, 86–90

Texas Education Agency, 87

Texas Hospital Association, 100

Thomason General Hospital, El Paso, 100

Torres, Isaias, 87, 91

Transnational identities, 30

Tucson University Medical Center, 98

Tucson Weekly (newspaper), 182

U

United Farm Workers, 144

The United States of Europe: The New Superpower and the End of American Supremacy (Reid), 148

United States (U.S.)
economy, 50–60
ethnic enclaves, 32, 35, 67
foreign-born population, 65
population growth, 72
underclass, 60
unemployment, 59–60
violent crime, 73

University Medical Center, Tucson, 98

University of California Medical Center at Irvine, 103

U.S. Chamber of Commerce, 144

U.S. Citizenship and Immigration Services (USCIS), 137

U.S. Customs and Border Protection, 118, 171

U.S. English, Inc., 13

U.S.-Mexico border, 96, 118–121, 149, 155, 168–169

U.S.-Mexico Border Counties Coalition, 96

V

Velasquez, Librado, 59–59

Vernon K. Krieble Foundation, 121

Villaraigos, Antonio, 46

Violent Crimes Institute, 50

Visas
H1-B, 68
H2-A, 111–112
Z Visa, 135–137, 139

W

Wage gaps, 43, 61–63

Washington, DC, 25

Washington Post (newspaper), 27, 42, 148

Washington state, 104

Welfare, 65

Welfare Reform Act (1996), 71, 75

Z

Zemikel, Mulu, 32–33

Z visa, 135–137, 139